Sourdough Starter for Beginners

Master the Art of Fermentation with Foolproof Recipes for Delicious Homemade Bread, Pizza, and Baked Goods

Table of Contents

Introduction

"Sourdough Starter for Beginners" is the book you're looking for to master the craft of sourdough baking. This incredible guide has something to offer to everyone. If you are new to sourdough baking, you will find helpful tricks and tips throughout the book to help you get the hang of this art in the easiest way possible. Or, if you're an expert, you will find enrichment in the amazing sweet and savory recipes provided in the book.

Sourdough baking has been around for a long time, and the bakers love it. The flavor, texture, and crispiness of sourdough bread are like no other, and why the bread has kept bakers hooked. Moreover, it is a fermentation process that is no less than a lab experiment. Sourdough baking will help you appreciate the science and art of making this bread.

It starts with plain flour and water and ends with a beautiful loaf of sourdough bread. These magic tricks or recipes are covered in this sourdough bible for beginners. Moreover, the book tells you all the tools and equipment you will need to bake confidently. You will find everything here, from learning about the key ingredients and how they are made, like sourdough starters, to managing fermentation.

This guide is easy to understand, simple, and great for beginners and experts. Everyone can benefit from this treasure of a book. It offers a hands-on approach and a step-by-step guide to help you navigate the sourdough baking process smoothly.

This guide was created with love and consideration for the readers. It consists of visuals, practical tips, and easy instructions, increasing your chances of excelling as a sourdough baker. You will learn many recipes, from baking the basic sourdough loaf to making pizzas, flatbreads, cookies, pancakes, and more.

"Sourdough Starter for Beginners" provides troubleshooting advice to help you deal with common misconceptions, challenges, and difficulties. This book aims to give you the confidence and motivation to learn and master the sourdough recipes.

So, don't wait. This exciting baking adventure awaits you to start creating your sourdough masterpieces. Do not hesitate. Allow yourself to become the baker of your dreams. Embrace the sourdough genius within you and start your fantastic journey as you read on.

Chapter 1: Introduction to Sourdough

Imagine taking a satisfying bite of freshly baked sourdough bread. Enjoying the complex flavors unfurling is like basking in the rewards of a day's hard work. Would you believe that the diverse flavors of this dough come only from a few simple ingredients? Essentially, you only need flour, water, salt, and some strategic planning to make sourdough. Yes, it's that simple.

The secret to the sourdough delectability is the magical interaction of bacteria and yeast. Once these spark the natural fermentation process, the bread develops its unique tangy aroma, and, after baking, the chewy crumb and the oh-so-satisfying chunky crust everyone loves.

1. *Sourdough bread is a widely popular choice among many bread lovers. Source: https://www.pexels.com/photo/brown-bread-600620/*

Sourdough, the world's first leavened dough, bridges cultures and traditions —the same way sourdough creates dynamic connections between different flavor profiles. This chapter introduces you to sourdough fermentation basics and the dough's versatility.

The Magic of Sourdough: Understanding Fermentation

The most magical aspect of making sourdough is that it's an entirely natural process. Unlike other breads, you won't need instant or other commercial yeast to make sourdough. Instead, you need a starter you made previously from flour and water. By making this starter, you're breeding your own microbial mix to leaven the bread. This, albeit promulgates the process, allows you to create a healthy product with natural ingredients (it even has natural preservatives).

How Fermentation Works

Fermentation is crucial for crafting a nuanced taste for your sourdough. So, in essence, it's an art, not a process. At the heart of the fermentation are the microbes that degrade and feed on the sugar from the flour. They produce lactic and acetic acid as a byproduct, which unlock the diverse flavors and act as preservatives. The longer the microbes can work their magic, the more complex the dough's flavor profile.

Besides the fermentation process, mixing, shaping, proofing, and baking contribute to the sourdough's texture, flavor, and smell. For example, the ratio of the combined ingredients affects how the microbes work through the sugars. Shaping can affect the dough's texture, while the proofing's duration can determine the tanginess of the finished bread. The final step in sourdough bread making is baking, bringing everything together, ensuring the rich flavors you've sparked during fermentation are captured in a delicious product.

2. *A sample of sourdough undergoing the process of fermentation.*
Source: PilotChicago, CC BY-SA 4.0
<https://creativecommons.org/licenses/by-sa/4.0>, via Wikimedia Commons.
https://commons.wikimedia.org/wiki/File:Sourdough_starter.jpg

Humidity, temperature, and the flour type influence the fermentation process. For example, depending on ambient temperature, the dough can take 4 to 12 hours to leaven (the warmer the temperature, the faster the process). By affecting these factors, you can adjust the timeline to your needs. Incorporating different flours will impact the timeline and the dough's texture and taste complexities.

Water is essential for successful fermentation as one of the three key ingredients. Achieving the delicate balance between texture, appearance, and taste is crucial. A higher water ratio means higher hydration and quick leveling. However, the dough might be harder to shape, so you might struggle to achieve the perfect texture despite the quick fermentation.

The Benefits of Fermentation

Did you know that sourdough has a higher nutritional profile besides tasting better? The anti-nutrients that prevent you from absorbing minerals from the flour are broken down during fermentation. As a result, the dough becomes more nutrient-dense and easily digestible.

The latter is the byproduct of the gluten breakdown. While beneficial for the dough's texture and structure, gluten is a resistant protein that gut microbes have difficulty digesting (even if you don't have gluten sensitivity). Fortunately, the microbes break the gluten down during fermentation so that sourdough will have fewer hard-to-digest molecules. Your digestive system will undoubtedly thank you for eating the light, airy sourdough.

During this microbial cooperation, yeast and lactic acid bacteria produce carbon dioxide, which causes the dough to rise. The unique combination of the microbes results in diverse depths of flavor, setting sourdough apart from commercial yeast-leavened bread.

3. Yeast plays quiet a big role in the production of sourdough. Source: https://pixabay.com/photos/baking-yeast-dough-bread-pastry-7395604/

To give you a crash course in fermentation microbiology, here is a breakdown of how the microbes do their magic. Yeast, these unique single-celled microorganisms, are fungi. Of the 1500 yeast species, only a few are used for fermentation. For example, the common baker's yeast (or Saccharomyces cerevisiae) gives the flavor basics for alcoholic brews and baked goods.

Yeasts fuel their reproduction cycle by feasting on simple sugars — like those in flour - known as alcoholic fermentation. After breaking down the sugars, the yeasts produce ethanol and carbon dioxide gas. This is aerobic respiration and is the same way people and many animals breathe — breaking down sugar and producing carbon dioxide.

While spreading through the dough, the gas creates bubbles, which become trapped in the dough between the gluten molecules, expanding it. As they keep reproducing, the yeast feeds on the available sugar, making more gasses and further improving the dough's power, aroma, and flavor profile. Higher temperatures (above 85°F) lead to faster yeast multiplication, producing an airy, spongy bread. Ethanol, a liquid at room temperature, evaporates into gas during baking, adding more bubbles to the dough's texture.

Other yeast species, like *Saccharomyces cerevisiae* or *Saccharomyces unisporus*, can contribute to the taste and texture diversity of the sourdough. Adding the former to your starter can achieve a lighter texture and tangier taste. The latter might be perfect for creating starters with higher hydration, resulting in an after-bread texture. Not surprisingly, there is a yeast species that produces artificial banana-smelling gas — perfect for banana bread enthusiasts.

Yeast also needs oxygen to work but can only absorb it gradually. Too much oxygen can prevent the yeast from working at a rate beneficial for the crumb texture and flavor —slow fermentation is beneficial here.

Combining the different yeast species is a great way to apply the divisibility of sourdough starter. However, yeasts are only one side of the coin for fermentation. On the other side are the good, lactic acid-producing bacteria (or LAB). Like many bacteria, they are everywhere around you in the environment (some believe the microbial flora on the baker's hand can impact the taste and texture of the sourdough). They are much smaller than yeast, but they're as important for dough making since there are more of them. Like yeast, lactic acid bacteria feed on simple carbs, except they produce lactic acid instead of gas.

Lactic acid is crucial for crafting the perfect sourdough for several reasons. It lowers the starter's pH, unlocking the dough's characteristic tangy flavor. Moreover, the low pH makes the dough an unfavorable environment for the bad microbes, preventing them from making the bread go off quickly. Lacto-fermentation lets you enjoy your delicious sour bread longer. Thanks to lactic bacteria, you won't have to worry about moldy bread — like commercially made bread, which goes bad quickly or is full of preservatives and unhealthy. The same principle (and bacteria) is used in making dill pickles, sauerkraut, and kimchi. Lactic acid bacteria break down gluten molecules, making the dough easier to digest.

Lactic acid bacteria can be homo-and heterofermentative. Thriving on temperatures from 86 to 95°F, Lactococcus, Enterococcus, Streptococcus, Pediococcus, and L. acidophilus are homofermentative and only make lactic acid. Used during fermentation, they produce light, tangy flavors, similar to yogurt or cream.

Besides lactic acid, heterofermentative lactic acid bacteria, like L. plantarum and L. fermentum, produce acetic acid, carbon dioxide, and ethanol. The latter two boost the dough's leavening power. They thrive at slightly lower temperatures (59 to 72°F) and, thanks to the acetic acid, yield a sharper, vinegar-like taste in doughs.

Sourdoughs typically contain more than one species of lactic acid bacteria (because you're introducing them from everyone in your environment). Each species will have different roles during fermentation. Those present initially will multiply quickly and help develop the dough's unique taste. Over time, their numbers fall and are replaced by species that provide an additional boost to the rise.

Hence, due to the shift in lactic acid bacteria colonies, the fermentation's duration affects the sourdough's flavor, texture, and stability. The longer it lasts, the sourer and airier the sourdough starter will become.

The finished sourdough starter is the byproduct of a complex chain reaction, which starts with the amylase enzyme activation. Amylase is naturally present in the flour, bacteria, and yeast but is inactive until you add water. As the wild yeast blooms, amylase activates and breaks down complex sugars in the flour. This is why high-hydration doughs are fluffier and airier. The more water, the faster amylase works through the sugars and produces gas.

Then, another flour enzyme, protease, breaks down the gluten protein molecules into peptides. Other enzymes break down the simple sugars, producing ethanol and carbon dioxide.

Breaking down gluten reduces the mixing time and increases water absorption speed. As the water becomes part of the dough, the peptides interact with the simple sugars, adding to the dough's color and flavor complexity. This process is crucial in distinguishing commercially leavened and quick-made sourdough (often falsely advertised as sourdough) from true, slowly leavened sourdough.

Why Is Sourdough a Unique and Versatile Bread Option?

Due to fermentation intricacies and the complex microbial dynamics involved in its creation, sourdough is a unique and widely versatile bread option. When you hear the word sour, you might understand the unique part but wonder how to enjoy this bread. It is a common question, especially if you're used to the taste and texture of bread produced with commercial leavening agents.

When you take a bite of these breads, what do you taste? You'll likely be hit with a more or a lesser sweet flavor, with a little alcohol-like sourness, like drinking beer (they don't call beer liquid bread for nothing!). It's a nice flavor, especially for breads like brioche — but it's also slightly monotone.

Biting into sourdough bread is an entirely different experience. Unlike those made with industrial baker's yeast, sourdough breads have a wider range of flavors within a single loaf. While sourdough is a little tangier in general — due to the natural presence of acids — its taste can vary depending on fermentation. You should aim for shorter fermentation for a sweeter, softer dough. In contrast, long fermentation is the way to go for a chewy texture and zestier flavor. Of course, you can choose something in between, playing with ratios, timing, etc., until you find the desired texture and flavor profile.

Due to the starter's microbial diversity, the bread is more aromatic and adaptable. In other words, you can combine it with a broader variety of food — from sweet to savory. For example, less tangy sourdough can have hints of a caramel or dairy flavor that goes well with sweet spreads. Dough with the sharper notes of wheat may pair well with savory ingredients like olive oil or vinegar.

The ways you can incorporate sourdough bread into your diet are nearly limitless. If you want more options to enjoy bread, sourdough is the solution. Whether you're a fan of traditional loaves, pizza, sandwich baguettes, or dinner rolls or experimenting with something more adventurous like dinner bread bowls, using sourdough won't disappoint you.

Regardless of the flavor delivered by the wild yeast and bacteria strains, the crunchy outer layer with the soft buttery inside makes the sourdough stand out from other bread options. However, don't worry if you prefer less crunchy. The diversity of sourdough allows you to create any inner and outer texture.

The characteristic flavor profile also contributes to the bread's popularity — once you share it with friends and family, rest assured you won't be the only one enjoying its benefits. The high-quality taste and satisfying flavor will captivate many - they'll be coming back for more.

Health Benefits

Besides using it for the bread you need or want, you'll gain other benefits from sourdough. One is the already mentioned easy digestibility due to low gluten content and unlocked minerals and vitamins —a lifesaver for those with gluten sensitivity. Some can't consume gluten at all. However, with sourdough, people with low to moderate gluten sensitivity can eat bread without buying pricey gluten-free commercial loaves.

4. *Not only is sourdough delicious, but it's also full of nutritious resources. Source:*
https://www.flickr.com/photos/treehouse1977/4587254073

During the slow fermentation process, more magnesium and zinc become available in the dough. Considering you can't get these from industrial yeast-leavened bread, sourdough is an easy way to add nutritional versatility to your diet.

Do you know what else makes sourdough nutritious? The lack of unnecessary ingredients. When you read the ingredients of commercially produced bread, you must go through a long list of additives, preservatives, sweeteners, flavor and texture changes, oils, and more. Beyond being completely unnecessary, these ingredients can lower the bread's nutritional quality. You won't have to worry about these additives with sourdough bread. You'll know what you're eating and the effects on your body and health.

Another reason sourdough is better is the breakdown of carbs. Simple carbs like those in industrially produced loaves spike blood sugar and cause them to drop as quickly. Sourdough microbes help prevent these spikes and falls by breaking down the sugars.

Lastly, and this might surprise you, sourdough can positively impact mental health. Making it requires practice and patience. It encourages you to slow down and concentrate on what you're doing, like mindfulness or meditation. You're creating something unique and alive while enjoying the activity's grounding effect. You add the ingredients, gradually feeding them to your starter, shaping the dough, and preparing it for the grand finale. Then, when your bread is finished, you bask in the fulfillment of making something beautiful and your own.

Unlike the usually uniform-looking commercial loaves, handmade sourdough bread is a joy to look at. They come in all shapes and sizes (depending on how you shape them) and become more aesthetically pleasing as they bake. You can carve intricate details onto the surface for those picture-perfect loaves.

Of course, the beauty of sourdough bread doesn't stop on the outside. While the yeasts and bacteria multiply, fermenting and producing gas, the dough becomes filled with bubbles. When cut in half, these bubbles create a cross-section akin to high-quality croissant dough.

The Excitement of Creating Your Own Sourdough Starter

Creating your own sourdough starter might not be the easiest process, but it's far more rewarding. As you gradually feed the starter with water, flour, or previous starter mix, you build excitement that culminates in the ultimate joy of baking your own healthy and delicious sourdough bread.

You can take your "fed" starter, divide it into portions, and feed them in a diverse ratio of ingredients. You can make only one type and discard the rest. Or you can play with the ratios and create a unique mixture you'll enjoy incorporating into various meals.

When you get the hang of creating the perfect mixture for your starter, you can toss in extra ingredients to enhance your sourdough bread flavors.

You'll be reminded, whichever route you go, that you're making something with your hands — and only from a few simple ingredients. When you take out the perfect loaf of bread from the oven and slice it into it, you'll see how rewarding the process will be.

You can consider making sourdough as a craft project or science experience, whatever suits your preferences. Both can be enjoyable and interesting, so it's only a question of finding the right approach. You will get through the inevitable ups and downs of this journey and finish and reap your rewards in a healthy, delectable loaf of homemade sourdough bread. As you embark on your sourdough journey, savor the taste and the marvel that unfolds within each slice.

Chapter 2: Embarking on Your Sourdough Journey

This chapter is about learning the basics of making sourdough bread. The tools and ingredients you will need before you begin your sourdough journey are explained. Making sourdough bread is an intricate art. Each ingredient has a science to it. Different ingredients yield different results. So, you must choose the right ingredients to get your desired results. You will learn what a sourdough starter is and how you make it.

Essential Ingredients and Equipment

Before beginning your sourdough bread-baking journey, consider what tools and equipment you need. You will be relieved to know that you do not have to spend a lot of money on baking supplies. You can also use your sourdough baking equipment in plenty of other recipes. You will probably already find them in your kitchen. Here is a list of tools and ingredients essential for baking sourdough bread:

Sourdough Starter

A sourdough starter is the most important component of your sourdough baking. The starter is a living culture of lactic acid bacteria and wild yeast that makes the bread rise. It is made by combining water and flour and letting it ferment. The sourdough starter differentiates sourdough bread from yeast-leavened bread. Making your sourdough starter will help you appreciate the intricacy of sourdough baking. You can buy a sourdough starter from the store. Either way, you must wait a few days before baking your sourdough bread.

Digital Scale

Whether baking sourdough or trying another recipe, measure your ingredients with a digital scale. They are better for accurately measuring your ingredients than other tools and aid you in making informed changes to the recipe based on the results.

5. *Digital scales are often very helpful in making sourdough, as they show precise measurements. Source:*
https://pixabay.com/photos/kitchen-scale-kitchen-scales-2442598/

Clear Containers

You can store your sourdough starter in ceramic, plastic, or glass containers. Using clear containers to accurately tell when the dough has risen is recommended. A glass container will help you see the starter's activity after it has been fed. The best thing about these containers is they come with a lid to cover the starter during its resting period. You can use two containers - one to store the extra starter in the fridge and the other for the current recipe.

Rice Flour

This flour helps with beautifying your bread. You can dust it on your baked bread once it's done. You can sprinkle it onto the pan before putting your dough on it to ensure it does not stick. Using rice flour is better than wheat flour as it burns at a higher temperature. It won't burn your dough.

6. *Rice flour helps enhance the appearance of your bread, also preventing it from burning easily. Source: https://unsplash.com/photos/person-holding-brown-bread-with-green-and-yellow-powder--xyyohpxxc8*

Bench Scraper

You must get a bench or a bowl scraper, especially when making sourdough bread. It will probably become your most used tool. You can use it to shape the dough, cut, turn, or keep it from sticking to the surface.

7. *To be able to cut and shape your sourdough as you wish, a bench scraper is required. Source:*
https://www.flickr.com/photos/mccun934/2290159427

Proofing Bowl

A proofing bowl has a large diameter of 8 to 10 inches at the opening and is usually made of organic materials. Once the dough is shaped, it is placed in the proofing bowl for the second rise, providing structure on the sides of the dough and keeping it in shape as it rises. You can line the bowl with a kitchen towel or dust it with rice flour to keep it from sticking as the dough rises. You can use any large bowl as a proofing bowl.

Bowl Covers

You must use silicone bowl covers to keep your dough covered as it rests in the bowl. The bowls can be used repeatedly and help keep the dough from drying. You can use plastic wrap plates or a damp flour sack towel to cover your dough in the bowl.

Bread Lame

A bread lame is a tool with a razor on one end to score the dough. Or you can use a sharp knife to slash the dough. The dough is cut to control where it expands. Otherwise, it may expand at its weakest point.

Dutch Oven

A Dutch Oven is a thick-walled cooking pot with a lid that fits tightly on the top. It bakes sourdough bread like a commercial steam oven - steam releases from the dough in the first few minutes of baking, giving the dough a better rise.

8. Using a Dutch Oven is vital to creating the perfect sourdough. Source: https://unsplash.com/photos/white-plastic-container-with-lid-ykqc-EWq9iQ

Parchment Paper

Parchment paper will help you transfer your dough from the work surface to the oven. It also keeps it from sticking to the pan.

9. Parchment paper prevents your dough from sticking, making the experience much smoother. Source: https://www.pexels.com/photo/woman-in-white-shirt-holding-a-pastry-brush-8290040/

Gloves

You should have long kitchen gloves to keep from burning yourself. Baking sourdough requires working in very hot temperatures, the long gloves protect your hands and arms.

Flour Varieties

A variety of flours can be used to bake sourdough bread. The most common flour is wheat flour. Other flours such as rye, spelt, or einkorn are also used.

10. The type of flour used can affect both the flavor and the texture of the dough. Source: https://pixabay.com/photos/bakery-bread-baker-apron-baking-1868396/

Wheat Flour

Wheat flour is divided into two: whole wheat and white flour. Whole wheat flour is produced by milling the wheat berries. It consists of about 15% protein content. Wheat flour is sifted to make white flour. Whole wheat flour has three main components: bran, endosperm, and germ. Bran is rich in fiber and adds flavor to the bread. It is the outer layer of the wheat berry. Endosperm is the innermost part of the wheat berry, and it is mainly made of carbohydrates, which are essential in gluten development. The germ is rich in fats and vitamins.

Wheat flour is sifted to remove the germ and bran, leaving only the endosperm. Bread made with white flour will have a mild flavor and softer texture. Whole wheat flour contains all the significant parts, so your bread will have a dense texture and be more complex than one with white flour. However, bran inhibits gluten formation, so it may not rise as much as one made with white flour.

Rye Flour

Rye flour consists of a complex fruit flavor and is popular among bakers. It has a lot of bacteria and wild yeasts, so sourdough starters made with rye flour are extremely popular. It has almost the same protein content as wheat flour, about 15%. However, you cannot make sourdough bread with only rye flour as it is difficult to knead. You must mix it with wheat flour for the best results.

Spelt Flour

Spelt flour is easy to digest and find. It has a slightly sweet, nutty flavor with a high protein content of around 17%. However, spelt flour is not as strong as wheat flour. It could result in a dense, flat loaf of bread if you bake your bread only with spelt flour. Using small portions of spelt flour with wheat flour to give your sourdough bread more flavor is recommended.

Einkorn Flour

Einkorn flour is the easiest to digest than other flours and also the simplest. It is known to be the earliest-grown wheat and has a very high protein content of 18% and a unique flavor. If you bake your bread only with einkorn flour, it may lead to a dense and crumbly loaf as it is not strong enough on its own. You must mix about ¼ of wheat flour with einkorn flour to make a more flavorful sourdough loaf.

All-Purpose Flour

You can make your sourdough bread with all-purpose flour. It will yield a soft, chewy, and crispy loaf. However, all-purpose flour does not have a high protein content, only about 11%.

You can use any flour that works best by trying combinations. Choose the flour that best suits your taste buds and has the right texture. Use all-purpose flour to stay safe as a beginner.

Choosing the Right Water

Did you know the water in your recipe could affect how your bread turns out? People usually think that drinking water will yield good bread if it is safe to drink. However, you would be surprised to know that this is not necessarily the case.

First is chlorination. If the water for your sourdough bread is chlorinated, it may affect yeast and bacteria growth in your bread. Nonetheless, it is not that common. If the chlorinated water has chloramines, the more persistent form of chlorine, it could interfere with the bacteria growth in your bread. You should contact your water supplier to determine how your water is treated.

The hardness of water may cause issues for some bakers. Water hardness is the mineral content dissolved in water and is measured in parts per million (ppm) or milligrams per liter (mg/l). You can contact your water supplier to find out the hardness of the water or do a home test with water hardness testing kits from the swimming pool supply companies. The best water for bread-making has a hardness of 50 to 150 ppm range. Anything less than this range means soft water and anything more suggests hard water. Soft water will yield a dough that is not cohesive enough. You may have soft water if your dough slacks or is too soft to hold shape. You can use more salt to make the gluten tougher. On the other hand, if you have hard water, then your dough will not be extensible. You can demineralize your water to soften it.

The pH or alkaline and acidity of your water can cause issues for baking. Dough made with water that is not as acidic is recommended. The dough can be unmanageable or soft with alkaline water. You can determine the water's acidity by contacting your water company or using a testing kit.

Another option is bottled spring water, which can be used to check if the problems persist. You must not use distilled water as it does not contain the important minerals for your sourdough.

Step-by-Step Guide to Creating Your Sourdough Starter

Your sourdough starter is the foundation for delectable sourdough bread. You can make your sourdough starter from scratch in a few easy steps. Once it shows consistent fermentation indicators every day, you will be ready to bake your sourdough bread.

Ingredients:

- 27 fluid ounces of water
- 14 ounces of whole-grain rye flour
- 10 ½ ounces of all-purpose flour

Instructions:

1. Add 3 ½ ounces of rye flour and 4 fluid ounces of warm water to a clean jar on day one.

2. Mix the ingredients and place them in a warm place for 24 hours.

3. On the second day, add 2.6 ounces of the mixture from the first day to another clean jar and discard the rest (Discarding Process)

4. Add 1.7 ounces of whole rye flour, 1.7 ounces of all-purpose flour, and 3.8 fluid ounces of water to the jar (Feeding Process)

5. Mix and store the jar in a warm place for 24 hours.

6. On the third day, add 2.6 ounces of the mixture from the second day to a clean jar and discard the rest.

7. Add 1.7 ounces of whole rye flour, 1.7 ounces of all-purpose flour, and 3.8 fluid ounces of water to the jar, mix, and store it in a warm place.

8. On the fourth day, you must feed your mixture twice. Add 2.6 ounces of mixture from the third day to a jar and 1.7 ounces of whole rye flour, 1.7 ounces of all-purpose flour, and 3.8 fluid ounces of water.

9. Mix the ingredients and let it rest for 12 hours.

10. After 12 hours, you must repeat the discarding and feeding process as before

11. Let the mixture rest overnight.

12. On the fifth and sixth day, repeat the discarding and feeding process with the same portion of ingredients as the fourth day. Do it twice a day.

13. On the morning of the 7th day, discard all jar contents down to 0.7 ounces of the mixture.

14. Then, add 1 ounce of whole rye flour, 2.4 ounces of all-purpose flour, and 3.3 fluid ounces of water.

15. Repeat this feeding process twice a day.

16. Repeat this process indefinitely until you want to keep the starter and start baking.

You do not have to use a new jar whenever you feed your starter. However, it does help to keep track of the jar's weight to understand how much mixture you have.

The Fermentation Process Explained

A little party of microorganisms begins when you add water to the flour and starter. When wild yeast and lactic acid bacteria are introduced to the flour's substrate, your dough comes to life. You can control this bacterial growth and activity by managing the hydration, temperature, and feedings. When you control the mixture's acidity, you control the rate enzymes break down the flour. Enzymes use bacteria to break down the food.

Yeast is divided into 2 groups: Saccharomyces and non-saccharomyces. They are versatile, can ferment sugars, and contain minerals, proteins, and vitamins. They can tolerate acidic environments with pH values of 3,5 or less. Hence, it can create a symbiotic relationship with the lactic acid bacteria.

Troubleshooting Common Issues

Why is the starter not rising?

The starter is a living culture, and each starter is unique. It will rise in its own time, and not every approach may work on your starter. There could be multiple reasons your starter is not rising, such as feeding frequency, hydration, temperature, ingredients, type, and flour quality. Your starter will rise better in warm temperatures between 75-85°F. Moreover, make sure your flour does not consist of chemicals.

What type of flour should be used for feeding?

You may use the same flour from which it is made for feeding. This way, you will form a consistent feeding routine, and the rise time will be more predictable.

How much flour and water to add?

You can use the ratio of 1:1:1 by weight for 100% hydration. This means adding 1 part starter, 1 part flour, and 1 part water.

Why is the starter not bubbly anymore?

This is completely normal, and there is no reason to panic. You must develop a consistent routine and repeat the feeding and discarding process for a few days for better results.

Does the jar have to be airtight?

It is up to you to keep your bowl covered loosely or airtight. Ensure the jar is large enough not to cause the mixture to burst out of the container if it is airtight. However, if you choose a loose covering, like a cloth, you may notice a layer forming on top of the mixture. Remove the layer and use an airtight lid if it bothers you.

Chapter 3: Nurturing Your Sourdough Starter

Once created, a sourdough starter requires constant nurturing to remain active — or to keep the yeast and bacteria alive. You can feed it with fresh flour, water, or another older starter to maintain its metabolic activity and produce flavorful byproducts. This chapter offers insight on feeding your sourdough starter and tips on keeping your starter happy and active.

Feeding Schedule and Techniques

When feeding your starter, stick to one key rule: all ingredients should be relative to the flour's weight of 100%. So, if you add half a cup of flour, you must add half a cup of water, too. The weight of the starter you're feeding should be around 20% of the flour's weight. With this, you'll have a little over a cup of starter every 4-12 hours, depending on ambient temperature. (You can alter the amounts - this is only an example.)

Depending on the flavor, texture, and activity you want to achieve, you can use the same flour type or mix two types to add to your starter. For example, all-purpose flour will take longer to induce metabolic activity than a whole rye-white flour mixture.

At room temperature (typically 76°F-82°F), you must feed your starter every 12 hours. If the temperatures are higher, the starter may ripen earlier.

- If you maintain a 12-hour feeding schedule, start when you see your initial starter is active. Plan to make it at a time so it ripens when it's convenient to start feeding it.

- When you add the flour, water, and starter, stir until you get a homogenous mixture, then cover the container to prevent air from getting in.

- Discard the rest of the starter by using it in your bread recipes. Experiment with the starter to see how it tastes and if you must adjust your feeding technique. Keep it in the fridge until you need it.

- Adjust the feedings depending on the temperature. For example, reduce the carryover starter amount during the warmer months to slow down the new starter's activation. This is great if you don't have the time to feed your starter every 4 hours. Conversely, you can raise the carryover amount during winter to kickstart the new starter's metabolic activity.

Feeding Schedule

While you can set your schedule, here is a sample to help you get an idea of feeding a starter:

- Your starter is active and ready to be fed at 10 AM. If you're keeping it at room temperature, you'll need to feed it again in 12 hours, at 10 PM.

- Add the flour and water at 10 AM when you feed a new starter.

- Check your starter in 2 hours, at noon. You'll see a slight activity, perhaps a few bubbles. You can smell it if you're curious, but it will likely smell like water and flour (unless it's warmer and the starter is more active).

- Recheck it in another 2 hours, at 2 PM. The starter should have expanded by about 100 %. If not, it may be too cold or need more flour or a starter.

- The mixture has lots of tiny bubbles by 5 PM, and the starter has acquired a slightly sour scent. It's increased in volume and might have a slight dome on top (it isn't flat).

- In two hours, at 7 PM, the top is flat or sunken in. The starter hasn't increased in volume but has larger bubbles on top. It needs a little more time before it's ready for another feeding.

- The starter ripens between 8 and 10 PM, acquiring a sour scent with a hint of sweetness. It's now full of big bubbles and holes that will give the perfect airy texture to your bread. So, feel free to use your discards to make bread.

- At 10 PM, take as much of the starter as you need and feed it with flour and water. Discard the rest.

Additional Tips

- If the ambient temperature is warmer (above 82°F), you must check the starter more often as it will likely ripen earlier. Adjust your feeding schedule accordingly if you don't mind increasing the frequency.

- The schedule doesn't have to be this strict. A 30-to-60-minute feeding time variant won't affect your starter too much.

- Additional ingredients may affect the feeding schedule, especially if they contain sugar. The microbes can multiply faster with more sugar, so your starter will ripen more quickly.

Maintaining the Right Environment

Maintaining a consistent environment is best - moderate to slightly warm temperatures to keep your starter alive and happy. Colder temperatures can make the microbes reluctant to multiply and send them into hibernation. Without the microbes, there is no fermentation and no active starter — your dough will not rise, and you'll have an unappetizingly flat and dense loaf. For the same reason, putting an active starter in the fridge is not recommended.

The ambient temperature will directly affect the bread quality. Nevertheless, you shouldn't expose your starter to direct heat as this could kill it (especially if the temperature is above 120 degrees).

Ensuring your starter is at a constant temperature, can be done in various ways: measuring its temperature with a probe thermometer, thermometer strips you put on the jar's outside, or a jar with a built-in thermometer. If the temperature is around 76°F, you're good to go, and your starter will thrive.

Your starter might need a bit of help warming up if the room temperature is below 76°F. Otherwise, it will become inactive or ripen extremely slowly.

11. *To achieve the texture you desire in the final product, leaving your starter in moderate to slightly warm temperature would be best. Source: https://unsplash.com/photos/brown-bread-on-white-and-black-surface-VoEoWHtNu-I*

Are you wondering how to keep your starter at the right temperature? Here are a few tips:

- Stick it in the oven with the lights on. It will have a warm and stable environment for ripening. Ensure you don't accidentally turn on the oven and cook your starter. This will not be the right option if you have an oven with only the lights on when turned on.

- Alternatively, if your oven has a defrost setting, this may work to keep your starter warm. Before trying it out, turn the oven to this setting and check the temperature to ensure it doesn't go above 82°F.

- Only add warm water when feeding. Warmer water will invigorate the microbes, activating their metabolism and keeping your starter alive. Put the container into a bowl of warm water if you fear the starter will cool down too quickly after adding warm water. The water you feed should not be warmer than 104°F and should be added slowly. The outside warming water can be warmer, up to 122 °F. When the warmth reaches inside the container, it will dissipate and won't cook your starter.

- If you have a big thermo-isolated cup, you can put some warm water in it, then place it in the starter to give it a helping hand. It's a good trick to keep the water temperature warmer over a longer period. You can do the same to slow your starter down by chilling it slightly.

- Use seed-raising mats or a specific heating mat made for fermentation. Both are a great option to infuse your starter with additional warmth during wintertime. Moreover, they won't take up much space because they are meant for busy kitchens. If nothing else, heating pads for sports injuries may also work.

- If you own a yogurt maker, you'll have another option to maintain the perfect environment for your sourdough starter. You can keep it at the optimal temperature, regardless of the ambient temperature. It will be outside of direct sunlight and thriving. Keep in mind that keeping it in the yogurt maker might make your starter grow exponentially, but this shouldn't affect its texture. If your machine has a timer, it's even better.

- Some instant pots have a yogurt-making setting. You can use it to keep your starter cozy and happy. If you have an instant or crock pot that doesn't have a yogurt setting, you can still use it, but without turning it on. Instead, place a mug of hot (it can be boiling) water next to the starter container, and cover it with the lid. It will create a warm environment without cooking the starter.

- Consider placing your starter on a higher shelf, fridge, or other elevated space (above the TV shelf if there's no other space) if the temperature in your kitchen is slightly below what is required. As hot air rises, it will accumulate at a higher level, providing the right temperature for your starter. Placing it on top of the fridge may provide additional warmth from the hot air circulating behind the appliance.

- Place your starter next to your oven if you use it often. For example, a higher cupboard shelf next to the oven would be a fantastic spot for your budding starter. It will get enough residual heat to remain active without the risk of cooking.

- Likewise, if you're making lots of tea during winter, keeping your starter next to the warm kettle will be a great way to keep it warm and happy.

- Another place to keep your sourdough starter warm is in the microwave. Putting your starter in the microwave and keeping the door slightly ajar (to keep the lights on without turning it on. Remember, don't cook your starter), you confine the heat generated by the microbial activity to a tight space. It works best if you've used warm water to feed it. Alternatively, put a mug of hot water or a heating pad next to the container inside the microwave.

- If you're afraid the warm water will be too much and make your starter ripen too quickly, wrap it in a thick, woolen sock (or a tea cozy) instead. Use lower-temperature water, and the sock will contain the warmth.

- If you explore other fermentation types, like kombucha, you can use a kombucha jar or pads to safeguard your starter and its microbial activity. Likewise, if you have a crock for making sauerkraut, you can place your sourdough inside. It will be insulated and kept warm to remain active.

- Keeping your starter in the car temporarily may also work, especially if your vehicle is parked in a sunny spot during winter. Check the inside temperature; cars can warm up more than you think. Underestimating the temperature may result in a quicker rise.

- Speaking of sunny spots, do you have a windowsill basking in the sun during the colder months? If so, this can be the perfect spot for your sourdough starter. The only caveat is that you must cover it with a cloth or wrap it up so it won't be exposed to direct sunlight. Also, don't do this during the warmer months because the temperatures will likely be much higher than required.

- If your temperatures are too high, you can prevent your starter from being overly active by placing it in a colder spot, like a lower shelf or on the floor.

- Alternatively, you can put it in a larger container with colder water. Avoid placing it in the fridge (as tempting as it sounds during summer when you want to avoid too frequent feeding) because this could deactivate the starter in a short time — unless this is your goal.

- Don't place your starter near the oven or other heat sources like a kettle if you keep it in the kitchen during summer. Likewise, don't put it under the AC as this can affect its temperature and humidity, drying up your starter.

While yeast dies at 140°F or above, your starter will begin dying long before it reaches this temperature. For the same reason, regularly checking its temperature, especially if providing a little extra warmth during the colder months, is crucial. The good news is that cooking is one of the few ways to kill a sourdough starter. If you can avoid this, you have a great chance of keeping your starter active and ready to make delicious bread.

While you are keeping your starter in a sealed container — the humidity will be mostly controlled — exposing it to overly high temperatures can affect it. The higher the temperature, the more the microbes absorb the moisture. Similarly, exposing your starter to direct sunlight or very strong artificial lighting can have the same effect. Keeping your starter in a dark space or covered (if it's near a direct light source) is advisable. As you've likely noticed from the storage suggestions, most provide coverage or a dark environment.

A sourdough starter can survive indefinitely under ideal conditions and with regular feeding. Note that a younger starter will require more frequent feeding (although this may depend on factors like flour, water temperature, etc.) to survive. You'll likely need to feed it every 12 hours to keep it alive. On the other hand, you can maintain a steady metabolic activity in a mature starter by feeding it every few days.

If you fail to keep your starter active, it will become inactive and lose its volume and bubbles. Also, it might become moldy and funky as the bad bacteria and fungi will take over and feed on it instead.

Signs of a Healthy and Active Starter

Now that you know how an inactive starter looks, you'll likely want to know how to recognize a healthy and active starter. Observe it closely — especially beginners, who may not know how to make the perfect mixture or maintain optimal conditions to establish a consistent feeding schedule.

A quick tip: Keep your starter in a see-through container so you can see what's happening inside.

Depending on the outside temperature, a new starter may take several days to activate. Albeit frustrating when you're eager to make your bread from scratch - this is normal.

Bubbles and Rising

After a few days, or maybe 24 hours if the temperature is higher, you'll see small bubbles forming on the starter's surface. You might notice a sour smell. The smell will likely appear later rather than sooner if it's colder. After a few more days, the bubbles will appear throughout the mixture.

12. Bubbles on the surface and an increased elevation level of the mixture are both signs of a healthy starter. Source: https://www.flickr.com/photos/andersknudsen/6718262487

Another Tip: Place a rubber band around the container to track how much it rises when activated. When the bubbles spread, the starter will rise, a sure sign of it being active and thriving.

Depending on the flour type, temperature, hydration, etc., your starter may or may not double in size. Some starters will rise to 100% in a few hours (especially in a warmer environment), and others will never rise this much — but this does not affect the dough's quality. However, using a specific dough to make it tangier and chewier can affect the activation and ripening times.

At lower temperatures, your starter may take longer to activate and rise but will eventually double in size.

As the bubbles spread, they might form a web-like structure (you can see this if you move the container and the mixture shifts slightly). If your starter acquires a spongy texture, it's highly active and close to being ripe.

A Pleasantly Tangy Scent and Aroma

An active sourdough starter will justify its name in smell and taste. Before activation, the mixture will have an overwhelmingly sweet smell and taste, which slowly disappears.

In a new starter, the smell can take up to 5 days to shift from sweet to sour, while in a re-fed starter, this can happen in as little as 5 hours. Either way, your starter should emanate unpleasant smells. If it smells too sweet after a few days or hours (depending on whether it's young or mature), it's likely not active, and the microbes might be dying and replaced with bad ones. This is the most likely scenario if the smell switches to funky or unpleasant.

Besides smelling it, consider tasting your sourdough starter. An active starter has a pleasantly sour aroma, like natural yogurt, and a little effervescent texture, like a beer or a fizzy drink.

Noisy Activity

Would you believe that an active sourdough starter can be quite noisy? All the bubbles forming and moving between the gluten molecules create lots of little popping sounds.

You won't hear this from afar, but if you put the container next to your ear and listen without other distracting sounds, you'll hear the magic happening. The bubbles rise to the surface, so hold the top of the container close to your ear.

Another sound to look out for is the hollow sound when tapping the bottom of the container. Gently tap it with your finger or a spoon to spark the noise activity.

Floating

The float test is a surefire way to determine if your sourdough starter is fully active. Scoop a tiny amount of dough and drop it in a bowl of water. If it floats on the surface, it's active and ready to be fed or used for baking, depending on whether it's a new or mature starter.

If it sinks, your starter isn't ready and needs more activation time. Remember that some starters may be ready and still not pass the float test due to their consistency. It doesn't mean they aren't good to be fed or used in baking. It merely means their texture makes them sink.

If these signs — the rising, the bubbles, the sizzling, and the pleasantly sour smell are there, your starter is active, regardless of whether it floats or not.

Loose Consistency and Softness

An active starter gradually acquires a looser consistency. From the stiff initial texture, it transforms into a mixture that shifts more easily in the container. You can verify this by lifting the container and slightly turning it to the side and back to see how quickly the dough moves.

Active starters are much softer than the initial ball-like dough you created. The starter's texture becomes creamier as the bubbles rise and travel to the surface, and the gluten protein transforms into peptides. When you stick your finger into it, it won't spring back but sinks into itself.

The Differences Between Liquid and Stiff Starters

Liquid and stiff starters may look slightly different when active. For example, a liquid starter will have more bubbles and a looser consistency. Depending on ambient temperature, it may activate sooner. It's highly hydrated, so microbial activity is increased.

Conversely, stiff starters may have fewer bubbles but a crackled texture. They rise slower and will likely have a dome-like shape initially.

A low-hydration starter may take longer to settle in the container. This is normal and doesn't mean it's not active. If it rises and acquires the tangy aroma, it's on the right track.

Chapter 4: Mastering Sourdough Recipes

This chapter goes a step forward and takes you through the recipes you need to become a professional sourdough baker. You will learn the intricacies of sourdough, from basic sourdough bread recipes to baking delicious sourdough pizza, muffins, and pancakes. So, buckle up, grab your kitchen mittens, and get ready to learn how it is done.

Basic Sourdough Bread

Baking sourdough bread requires more than a simple recipe – it involves understanding. As you now know, sourdough bread is made with a natural leavening agent instead of commercial yeast. This sourdough bread recipe will give you a crisp, chewy loaf with a tangy flavor and a crackly crust. It is healthier than your supermarket bread, easily digestible, and more delicious. For this recipe, you will need simple ingredients, time on your hands, and patience.

13. After you taste its rich sourness and soft texture, the sourdough bread will be a regular in your diet. Source: https://www.flickr.com/photos/mwf2005/8742390414

Ingredients:

- 3 ½ ounces of active and bubbly starter

- 11 fluid ounces of water

- 1 lb. of all-purpose flour

- 2 1/3 tsp of salt

Instructions:

1. You must feed your starter 4 to 12 hours before starting your dough to ensure it is active and bubbly.

2. Mix the water, active starter, flour, and salt in a large bowl with a wooden spoon or with your hands.

3. Cover the bowl with a lid or plastic wrap and let it sit for 30 minutes to ensure the water hydrates the flour.

4. Now, stretch and fold your dough. Start by grabbing one end of the dough and pulling it upwards to stretch it out.

5. You may have to bounce the bread to get it to stretch.

6. Bring the pulled end back to the center.

7. Give your bowl a quarter turn and stretch and fold your dough again.

8. Repeat the process twice to complete one round of stretching and folding.

9. Let the dough rest for 30 minutes, and complete one more round of stretching and folding.

10. Cover the bowl for another 30 minutes and allow it to rest.

11. Finish the last round of stretch and fold, then cover your bowl with a plastic wrap, lid, or a damp kitchen towel.

12. Allow it to rest in a warm place for about 6 to 12 hours until it doubles in size.

13. Do not let it over-ferment.

14. Dust the work surface with flour and place your double-in-size dough on it.

15. Fold the dough onto itself, roll it up, and spin it towards you until it is shaped into a ball.

16. Let the dough sit for 15 to 20 minutes without covering to keep it from sticking to the tea towel during its overnight rise.

17. Fold two sides into the middle and pinch them together.

18. Repeat the process on the other two sides to create a surface tension in your dough.

19. This will lead to a good rise.

20. Place the dough in a floured bowl dusted with rice flour or all-purpose flour to keep it from sticking, and cover it with a tea towel.

21. Cover the bowl with plastic and place it in the refrigerator for 12 to 15 hours, or allow it to rest at room temperature for 3 to 4 hours.

22. Preheat your Dutch oven for 1 hour at 500°F.

23. Remove the dough from the fridge when ready to bake and put it on parchment paper.

24. Dust the dough with flour and slash the top with a razor to give it a big expansion score and cute designs.

25. Place the dough with parchment paper into the hot Dutch oven and cover it with the lid.

26. Put the Dutch oven in the hot oven.

27. Let it bake for 20 minutes before removing the lid with your mittens.

28. Turn the oven temperature down to 475°F and let it bake for 15 to 20 minutes until golden brown.

29. Take it out and let it cool down.

30. Enjoy!

Tips:

1. Ensure you use an active sourdough starter

2. It is normal for the dough to seem dry when it first comes together. You can use wet hands for stretching and folding if the dough is too sticky.

3. The time it takes your dough to double may vary depending on various environmental factors, such as temperature, hydration, and the starter's maturity.

4. Use a kitchen scale for accurate results.

Mixing and Kneading

Although mixing and kneading were discussed in the recipe, they deserve to be discussed a little more. After all, this process leads to proper gluten development, a good dough structure, and the retention of bubbles in your dough once it is baked. Mixing and kneading fall under the aggressive dough handling category. These initial stages require combining ingredients and developing gluten. Mixing integrates the raw ingredients. Kneading requires you to manipulate the dough to make it more homogenous and to promote gluten development. There are various ways you can knead, such as:

Hand Kneading

Hand kneading is the most reliable kneading technique. It requires pushing and mashing the dough on the counter with the heel of your hand. You can stretch the dough towards you and fold it in the center while rotating the bowl to ensure you maintain a circular shape. It helps your dough maintain a consistent shape. This process requires much hard work and physical labor. The more force you apply, the faster your dough will come together and develop gluten more quickly.

Mechanical Mixing

You can use a mechanical mixer if you do not want to exert yourself by hand kneading. This method helps you mix the dough in a shorter time frame. Also, it leads to full gluten development. However, there are some drawbacks to mechanical mixing. If you knead the dough in the mixer for too long, it can break the bonds between the gluten proteins. An overmixed dough becomes slack, lacking elasticity, and will not hold its shape. Moreover, it could aerate the dough too much, causing oxidative damage and losing its color and flavor. Different breads require different kneading styles, which may not be possible to manage with a machine. Hand mixing allows you to pay attention to the dough and is a much gentler process.

Proofing and Baking

Proofing bread dough is when the dough is given its second rise or final fermentation or shape before it is placed in the Dutch oven. The dough will continue to ferment during proofing to build more acidity and increase volume. It is important not to confuse proofing with bulk fermentation. The proofing stage takes place just before baking the bread when the dough has been shaped into its final form. It occurs when the dough has been divided into smaller pieces, shaped, and placed in the proofing container. The sourdough's proofing temperature depends on the quality, texture, and flavor you desire. The two proofing types are same-day proofing in warm temperatures (1 to 4 hours) and cold proofing (retarding) for many hours or overnight.

As your bread is proofing, preheat your oven to 500°F with a Dutch oven inside - this is for the steam. Once your bread is proofed and your Dutch oven is heated, it is time to bake your dough. Place your dough in the Dutch oven, then carefully place it in the oven. Be careful not to burn your fingers. When you place your dough in a Dutch oven, the water from the dough will turn into steam, which is captured in the oven. Humid environments help develop a light brown, glossy, and crisp crust.

Beyond Bread: Sourdough Pizza Crust and Flatbreads

You can make incredible pizzas and flatbread with your sourdough starter. Everyone loves pizza and the sauce's tomatoey goodness. However, pizza made from sourdough crust hits differently. It has a fabulous texture and is more flavorful and healthier. It is easy to digest thanks to the long overnight rest your sourdough gets because it helps break the glutenous enzymes, eventually making digestion faster.

Sourdough Pizza Crust

14. The sourdough pizza crust is a favorite for sourdough lovers. Source: https://unsplash.com/photos/pizza-on-black-round-plate-PJ_NtTm4btA

Ingredients:

- 8 ½ fluid ounces of water
- 1.7 ounces of active sourdough starter
- 1 2/3 tsp of fine sea salt
- 12 ½ ounces of bread flour
- Pizza toppings of choice

Instructions:

1. Mix the water and sourdough starter with a fork in a large bowl and add salt and flour.
2. Continue mixing. Use your hands to ensure the flour is fully incorporated.
3. Cover the dough with plastic wrap or a kitchen towel.
4. Allow it to rest at room temperature for 30 minutes.
5. Then, stretch and fold the dough over itself a few times and shape it into a ball.
6. Place the dough in an oiled bowl and cover it.
7. Let the dough rise overnight at room temperature for about 10 to 12 hours until it is doubled in size.
8. Oil the baking pan using olive oil.
9. Put the dough into the pan directly and stretch it out until it reaches the pan's sides and corners (the dough will naturally spread out if it is relaxed or may resist, which is common after a long rise).
10. Cover the pan with a baking sheet and let it rest in a warm place (78°F) for 30 minutes.
11. Dimple the dough again as you did before by stretching and lifting it.

12. Cover it for another 30 minutes and preheat your oven to 450°F.

13. Par-bake the crust after 30 minutes.

14. Place the pizza pan on the bottom rack and bake it for 15 to 18 minutes or until the bottom crust is light golden brown at 450°F.

15. Use tongs to check the bottom of your dough.

16. Remove the pan from the oven when done.

17. Place toppings of your choice on the par-baked pizza crust.

18. Add seasonings and cheese.

19. Place it on the middle or top rack and let it bake for 450°F.

20. Let it bake until the cheese is melted for 12 to 15 minutes.

21. Remove from the oven and serve hot.

Tips:

1. Put the pizza crust on a cooling rack and let it aerate so that the crust does not become soggy if you want to store it for later. Then, cover it tightly with plastic wrap and let it rest for 6 hours at room temperature. When ready to bake, place it in the same pan and follow the above instructions.

2. You can line the pan with parchment paper to ensure the dough does not stick.

3. Focus on your crust rather than the time - every oven and dough are different, and your baking conditions will vary.

4. Use good quality whole-milk mozzarella cheese and not bagged cheese, as it has agents that may destroy your pizza.

5. Use room temperature to make sure the pizza crust is crisp.

Sourdough Flatbread

Sourdough flatbreads are light on the stomach, easy to make, and delicious. This recipe is perfect for making wraps, eating with gravy, and when warm. This bread is chewy, flavorful, and soft. Sourdough flatbreads are a must-make.

15. If you want an easy-to-digest, healthy, and delicious treat, then sourdough flatbread is the way to go. Source: https://pixabay.com/photos/italian-cuisine-flatbread-food-1047388/

Ingredients:

- 1.9 ounces of all-purpose flour
- 6 fluid ounces of warm water

- 6.1 ounces of active sourdough starter

- 2 tbsp of olive oil

- 2 1/3 tsp of salt

Instructions:

1. Combine olive oil, flour, water, salt, and sourdough starter in a large bowl and mix with a wooden spoon.

2. Use your hands to bring the dough fully into shape.

3. Knead using the stretch and fold method a few times to shape the dough into a ball.

4. Cover the bowl and let the dough rest for 2 to 6 hours at room temperature until it doubles in size.

5. Dust flour on parchment paper and put it aside.

6. Then, divide your dough into ten equal portions of about 2.3 to 2.6 ounces each.

7. Shape these portions into a ball by turning the ends underneath.

8. Space them apart on parchment paper.

9. Let it rest for 30 minutes.

10. Then, dust your workspace and roll each portion into a thin 7-inch circle - it does not have to be perfect.

11. Cook your flatbread on a preheated griddle for 1 to 2 minutes each, or use a hot skillet.

12. Cook each side until golden.

13. Bubbles may form as it cooks. Do not burst the bubbles.

14. Serve the flatbread warm with meals or make sandwiches.

15. You can store the dough in a bag in the refrigerator or freezer.

Sweet Treats: Sourdough Pancakes, Muffins, and More

With your sourdough starter, you can make breakfast must-haves like pancakes, waffles, muffins, etc. This section provides basic recipes to treat yourself to a healthy, sweet breakfast.

Sourdough Pancakes

This sourdough pancakes recipe is the perfect breakfast option if you want something sweet to start your morning while caring for your health. These pancakes are light on the tummy and won't make you feel sleepy after consuming them. If you have a sourdough starter, this recipe only takes 10 to 15 minutes. You can make it on the same day or overnight and save the leftover pancake batter for later.

Ingredients:
- 3.7 ounces of all-purpose flour
- 8 ½ ounces of sourdough starter (active and bubbly)
- 2 tbsp of sugar
- 2 large eggs
- 8 fluid ounces of milk
- 2/3 tsp of fine sea salt
- 5 ¼ tsp of baking powder

- 2 2/3 tsp of baking soda

- 3 1/3 tbsp of melted unsalted butter or oil

- Toppings of choice

Instructions:

1. Add all the dry ingredients except the baking soda and baking powder to a large bowl and add the wet ingredients.

2. Mix them well.

3. Cover the bowl and let it rest overnight.

4. Add the baking soda and powder to the bowl the next morning and mix again.

5. Your batter's texture will be bubbly, thick, and pourable. Add extra milk to thin out the mixture (1 tsp at a time) if needed.

6. Let the batter sit for 5 minutes before cooking.

7. Preheat your skillet to medium-low and coat it with butter.

8. Put ⅓ cup of batter on the pan and cook each side for 1 to 2 minutes.

9. Wait until bubbles form and the edges puff up.

10. Flip it over and let it cook for another minute or so.

11. Place the pancake on a plate.

12. Serve with your favorite toppings.

16. *The sourdough pancake, especially when served with maple syrup, is an extraordinarily delicious dessert. Source: https://pixabay.com/photos/pancake-breakfast-food-dessert-7811889/*

Sourdough Muffins

Sourdough muffins are a great sweet treat if you want something not as sweet as regular muffins with a different but tasteful texture and flavor. You can add syrup or toppings of your choice. They can be stored for two days at room temperature on your countertop.

Ingredients:

- 1.7 ounces of granulated sugar
- 8 ounces of all-purpose flour
- 8 ounces of sourdough starter
- 12 fluid ounces of milk
- 1 ½ tsp of baking powder
- ¼ tsp of salt

- 1 tsp of vanilla extract

- 4 ½ tbsp of melted butter

- 1 large egg

17. The sourdough muffins are a perfect choice for a quick or on-the-go snack. Source: https://unsplash.com/photos/white-ceramic-plate-with-muffins-ldUMCsT7iFU

Instructions:

1. Preheat your oven to 350°F.

2. Coat your mini muffin tin with oil and put it aside.

3. Mix the dry ingredients in a medium-sized bowl.

4. Mix the wet ingredients in a small bowl.

5. Add the wet ingredients into the dry ingredient bowl and mix well.

6. Let the mixture sit for a few minutes (3 to 5 minutes).

7. Pour the batter into the muffin tin, filling in each slot.

8. Bake for 17 to 20 minutes.

9. Check if the muffins are well cooked by inserting a toothpick and checking if it comes out clean.

10. Serve with your favorite toppings.

Tips:

1. Mix the dry ingredients well when you add the wet ingredients to avoid clumping.

Sourdough Chocolate Chip Cookies

You can make delicious chocolate chip cookies using your sourdough discard. The cookies are chewy, soft, and thick. You can store the dough in your fridge or freezer to ensure your cravings are always satiated.

18. Sourdough chocolate chip cookies are enjoyed by many people, especially children. Source: https://www.pexels.com/photo/baked-cookies-on-table-2377472/

Ingredients:

- 3.3 ounces of all-purpose flour
- 4.4 ounces of bread flour
- 1 large egg
- 4.4 ounces of sourdough starter
- 1 ¼ tsp of vanilla extract
- 4 ounces of unsalted cold butter
- 1 ¼ tsp of sea salt
- 3 ½ ounces of light brown sugar
- 3 ½ ounces of white granulated sugar
- 12 ounces of chocolate chips
- 1/3 tsp of baking soda
- 2/3 tsp of baking powder

Instructions:

1. Mix all dry ingredients in a bowl with a fork and put it aside.

2. Mix eggs, vanilla extract, and sourdough starter in a separate bowl until they turn into a smooth batter and put it aside.

3. Add the cold butter and brown and white sugar to a stand mixer.

4. Beat on low speed for a minute until it turns into small crumbles.

5. Add the chocolate chips and mix on low speed for 45 seconds.

6. Empty the mixture into a separate large bowl.

7. Add the dry ingredients and mix on low speed for 30 seconds until it becomes crumbly.

8. Add the egg mixture and mix it on low speed until the dough forms.

9. Stir the batter and make sure you have added all the ingredients.

10. Divide the dough into 12 portions and put them on the parchment paper-lined baking tray.

11. Cover the tray and let it rest for 2 hours in the refrigerator, or let it rest for 24 hours for the best results.

12. Bake the cookies in a preheated 375°F oven for 15 to 18 minutes.

13. The cookies should be golden brown or until the center appears slightly undercooked.

14. Remove the tray from the oven and let it rest for 5 minutes before transferring the cookies to a cooling rack.

15. Serve and enjoy!

Tips

1. You can store the cookies in a jar at room temperature for up to 7 days.

2. Put a piece of white bread in the jar to keep the cookies fresh.

3. You can freeze the uncooked cookie dough for up to 3 months.

4. You may use all-purpose flour in place of bread flour. However, making cookies using only all-purpose flour yields less chewy cookies.

Chapter 5: Troubleshooting and Tips for Success

Sourdough making isn't hard, but reaching perfection can be challenging, especially tailoring the dough for existing recipes. Mistakes can cost you time, flour, and energy. This chapter provides tips on common errors in sourdough baking to help you avoid these losses.

For assistance, you'll also receive tips for adjusting recipes to your preferences, along with guidance to perfect your sourdough masterpieces.

Common Challenges in Sourdough Baking

Baking Too Soon

One of the biggest errors novice bakers make is baking their sourdough too soon. Remember, a starter needs a few days to reach that perfectly leavened dough (unless it's mature). Even if your starter isn't new, you want it more than just bubbly. So, be patient and wait a little while before baking it.

When trying your new starter in a recipe, use the discards for simple dishes like pancakes. Otherwise, wait a few days, even after you notice the bubbling and strong but pleasant tangy smell.

Using the Wrong Water

The water can make or break your sourdough baking success. You're welcome to use tap water, but it must be filtered. Unfiltered water can contain chlorine, which will suffocate your starter's microbial activity. The result will be a flat, dense dough without bubbles.

Leave the water for the starter in a bowl for at least 24 hours before use if you don't have a filter. The chlorine will evaporate, and your baked goods will be airy thanks to increased yeast and bacteria activity.

Likewise, too hot or cold water can deter microbial activity and prevent your dough from rising to its full height. Use room temperature water for feeding and dough baking.

Being Impatient

Being impatient will prevent you from achieving the perfect texture and flavor in your sourdough recipes. Besides not baking too soon (to ensure extensive fermentation can occur), developing a strong baking routine is a good idea. Build this around your needs, experience, desired recipe, and technique, and you'll have enough time to avoid rushing the dough-making and baking.

For example, determine when you want your dish ready. Then, calculate how long it will take to get through all the steps — the feeding, fermentation, proofing, etc.

Having dough ready 24-72 hours before the final proofing is another way to ensure the sourdough is ready precisely when you need the bread, pizza, or whatever you're making.

Skipping Autolysis

Autolysis is crucial for a good rise in sourdough, especially if you're baking bread. When combining the starter with water and flour, wait 45 minutes before adding the salt. During this time, autolysis happens, flour hydrates, and the dough leavens. Then, add the salt and proceed with the rest of the pre-baking steps.

Not Letting Gluten Develop Properly

Sourdough contains less gluten due to the slow natural fermentation and the lack of hardcore kneading. However, some gluten is needed for the characteristic sourdough bread texture and density.

If you are unsure whether your dough has enough gluten before baking, stretch a small piece between your fingers. If you can stretch it to the point of becoming see-through (transparent) without breaking, your dough has enough gluten. If it breaks, your dough is not gluten-ready.

Gluten development can be tricky with whole-grain flour (they have less natural gluten), so you need to be more patient with them. Conversely, letting them develop enough gluten will help your whole-grain dough form much nicer, delicious loaves.

Not Proofing Long Enough

Exercising patience is a theme in sourdough baking. When you've waited for days for your starter to activate and the dough to rise and gone through the numerous steps of preparing it for baking, you might be tempted to skip some of the proofing time and get your bread in the oven.

Baking underproofed dough is a recipe for disaster. Your bread might remain dense and damp — or have long tunnels where the air bubbles connected before dispersing through the dough and rising to the surface.

Different doughs require diverse proofing times, so you must read their cues to determine whether they are ready. For most sourdough breads, 2 - 4 hours of cold proofing should be sufficient, but checking before baking is recommended.

The finger poke test is an easy way to check if your dough is proofed. Dig your fingers into it. If they leave an impression without the dough springing back, your dough is ready to bake.

Not Forming the Bread Properly

If you ended up with a bread flat as a pancake, you've likely not formed your dough properly. This is one of those crucial pre-baking steps you don't want to skip because it creates surface tension on the dough's outer layer, ensuring your loaf expands upwards.

One of the most foolproof methods to form the bread is to pull it against the natural traction of your countertop. The goal is to stretch the dough's outer layers until they become taut. Repeat the pulling motion until your dough sits in one place on the countertop without clumping or spreading toward the sides.

Not Scoring the Surface

You might not be ready to try intricate scoring designs, but you don't want to skimp on proper scoring. If you do, your bread will be distorted or burst along the sides due to the last push of rising energy while baking.

To help the energy come to the surface naturally without disfiguring the bread, score the dough deeply enough to cut through the outer layer and into the inner core (about half an inch). Do it with a sharp knife so it leaves clean edges when splitting.

Underbaking

No one likes doughy bread, but this will happen if you don't bake it long enough. Do the thump test to ensure your loaf is fully baked. Turn it over and thump the bottom with your knuckles. Does it sound hollow? If so, it's ready. Otherwise, it needs a little more baking.

19. For perfect texture and taste, the bread should be left in the oven at a certain temperature long enough. Source: https://www.pexels.com/photo/man-reaching-into-the-over-for-bread-11952100/

Use a meat thermometer if you want to be more confident in your bread's readiness. It's fully baked at an internal temperature of 200°F.

Not Letting the Bread Rest

Cutting into the warm, freshly baked loaf can be as tempting as putting it in the oven too soon. You should resist this at all costs. Proper cooling is the final step of the baking process (not only to avoid burning your mouth).

When you take the bread out of the oven, its interior is still cooking (remember it should be around 200°F). The moisture continues to evaporate, helping the characteristic texture to form. If you cut into it before the cooking process is finished, you may end up with a slightly different texture.

If you enjoy warm sourdough bread, you can reheat it slightly after it has cooled and completed baking. Toss it in the oven for 10 minutes at 350°F, and it will be as delicious as if you've just baked it.

Not Using Discards

One of the best things about making sourdough is getting more dough for baking — if you don't throw away your discards. Some sourdough recipes work perfectly with unfed discards. So, why would you not take advantage of this?

Improper Storing

Did you know that properly storing your baked goods can save you plenty of baking time, energy, and resources? For example, storing uncut bread in a paper bag or bread box prevents it from going stale or moldy, ensuring you can enjoy it for longer. Likewise, storing cut loves in the freezer can help you stack up on bread when you don't have time to bake new loaves.

If you store bread in the freezer, wrap it in plastic wrap, foil, or a Ziploc bag to prevent dehydration. When it thaws, run water over the crust, place it in the oven at 350°F, and re-bake it for 10 minutes.

If your bread gets a little stale (which, thankfully, takes a long time for sourdough), you can use it for croutons, bread pudding, breadcrumbs, etc.

Adjusting Recipes to Fit Your Preferences

Starting with 100% hydration starters (equal amounts of flour and water) is recommended for beginners adjusting existing recipes. Add more water and flour to the recipes you want to tailor. Some will be tricky if they're usually low hydration. Others are easier, but you'll always need to account for the additional water and flour.

The number of starters you need depends on what you're making. As a general rule of thumb, start with ½ cup water and flour to ⅔ cup of starter - this will likely be enough to leaven your dough properly. If you want it to be airier and sour-tasting, add a little more starter.

Once you know how much starter you need, subtract the amount of water and flour from the other liquid and flour in your recipe. For instance, if you added ½ cup of starter, deduct ¾ of a cup of liquid and ¾ of a cup of flour.

Combine everything and see if you need to make adjustments (adding more liquid or flour). Note these down for future reference.

Adjusting the additional fermentation time during proofing further tailors your dough to the recipe. For example, about 4 hours of extra fermentation will be enough if you want a rustic dough. For a richer dough, proofing is required for 8 or more hours (overnight or an entire day).

Conversely, if your recipe doesn't require rising (like a pie or cookie), you can reduce the 4 hours of room temperature proofing.

Consider a bread recipe with 3 cups of flour, 1 cup of milk, and 1 ⌧ cup of water as a more precise example and the easiest tailing method. You add 8 ounces of ready-to-go starter, so you must deduct 4 ounces of liquids and 4 ounces of flour. You can remove the water and reduce the milk by 2 ounces to eliminate the liquid. The result will be a rich but not too sour bread with enhanced natural flavor.

If you want to make a cake recipe requiring 8 ounces of water and 6 ¼ ounces of flour, start with 7 ounces of starter (discards can work for cakes, too). Reduce the water and flour in the recipe by 3 ½ ounces each, mix, and bake until you get a delicious, airy cake.

As you can see, you can tailor sourdough to many different recipes — whether fed and ready-to-go starters or unfed discards. The only caveat is that the existing recipe must include enough fluids and flour to substitute the starter.

However, if you substitute milk, you lose fat and solids, which enhances the bread's texture and flavor. For the same reason, choose recipes that require water or water and milk combo — unless you don't mind making the tradeoff. Moreover, milk fats and solids aren't necessary for some bread (even if they're in the recipe) but are only added for extra fluffiness. If you don't mind the rustic aesthetics, feel free to substitute them.

Expert Tips for Perfecting Your Sourdough Creations

Do you wonder how to achieve the perfect sourdough success every time? Below are a few expert tips to help you:

Get the Right Consistency

If your dough is too thin, it won't rise properly because the bubbles will escape the structure. The best way to avoid this is to thicken your dough with high-protein flour. This is particularly recommended for high-hydration doughs as these often become runny with beginners' hands. Even if your recipe requires a moist dough, it must be slightly gloppy and not pourable before proofing.

In contrast, if your dough isn't properly hydrated, it will be too stiff to let the bubbles rise to the surface. The solution is adding more water.

Cooling the Dough

It's much easier to score chilled dough. Store the dough in the fridge for a couple of hours to make an intricate design. You will have more time to work without the dough becoming too mellow (you could accidentally smash it while scoring).

Moreover, the lines on refrigerated dough will come out much nicer after baking. They will be clean-cut and produce your beautiful design.

Letting the dough sit in the fridge overnight is more convenient if you work with a tight schedule. You're doing the dough-making and folding one day and the carving and baking the next.

Learn to Work with High-Hydration Dough

High-hydration doughs are always challenging for beginners. Here are a few ways to make it easier:

- Gently pull the dough towards you, then fold it in the bowl. Continue until the dough doesn't stick to your hands as much.

- After folding, let it sit for a few minutes.

- Wet your hands with water and remove the dough from the bowl. Shape it by pulling it slightly between your hands. Put it down and wet your hands again when it starts sticking to your hands.

- Gently squeeze the dough between your fingers a few times to make it stronger (enhancing gluten formation).

- Sprinkle the work surface and the proofing dish with rice flour before the final shaping and proofing.

Preheat the Dish

Putting the dough into a cold baking dish can cause it to flatten while it heats up in the oven. This could alter its texture and the design you created during scoring. To prevent this, preheat the dish before scoring. Once scored, the dough should go straight to baking.

Use a Sharp Tool

Using a very sharp tool when scoring is imperative. Sharpen a knife beforehand. There are specific bread knives for this purpose — although nothing truly beats the good old razor blade. You can't go sharper than a razor blade, and you'll control to make even the most intricate designs.

Sprinkle the Loaf with Flour

Do you want your design to look even more beautiful? Sprinkle the dough with flour before storing it. The flour will make the contrast stand out as your dough rises and splits.

20. Sprinkling some flour on your dough will enhance its final appearance. Source: https://www.pexels.com/photo/chef-making-dough-for-cookies-in-bakery-6287300/

Moisten the Dough's Surface

Do you struggle with flat, unappetizing bread despite making your dough according to the recipe? If so, your dough may need a little additional moisture. Sprinkle it with water before baking - this is how professional bakers get those perfectly shaped and risen loaves every time.

Use a generous amount of water to keep the dough flexible enough to withstand the pressure of the bubbles rising inside. Your loaf will rise longer while baking.

Put a couple of ice cubes next to your dough in the baking dish to get an even moister loaf. The ice will immediately melt in the preheated dish, creating steam to help you get the perfect oven spring.

Handle Your Dough Gently

One reason sourdough-making became popular is that it doesn't require aggressive kneading. You can only get a light and airy texture if you preserve the gas developed during the previous phases. Aggressive handling would defeat this purpose because it would push out all the bubbles.

Knead the dough gently, with light pushing and folding movements to preserve the bubbles. Don't punch or push down on it hard if you don't want to waste the precious ripening and proofing time.

Use Sifted Flour

Sifting flour adds a light texture to sourdough, further enhancing its airiness. Work with whole-grain flour will have heavier parts that may weigh down your bread, preventing it from becoming fluffy and perfectly crumbly.

Sifting flour removes these parts so they won't weigh down and hold up air through the dough's texture. Your bread will have a nicer crumb and overall structure because the bubbles can rise between the gluten molecules without obstruction.

Soak Your Flour

Do you want an even lighter dough? Soak your flour before adding it to the dough. This method has a similar effect to sifting — preventing the flour's heavy parts from interfering with gas formation.

Soak the flour overnight; the heavy parts will become soft enough to let the bubbles pass around them and rise to the surface. They become flexible, so they won't severe the gluten strains. You'll have many air pockets and the perfect crumb every time.

Add Water

Are you worried your bread won't be soft and airy enough? When in doubt, simply add more water. The more water, the larger holes you'll have in your crumb, and the bread's texture will be milder, too.

Alternatively, add less flour if you're having another go at a recipe where the bread wasn't soft enough on the previous try. It's the same as adding more water, except you will work with different proportions.

See whether you can handle the dough when preparing it for baking. Albeit yielding a magically airy bread, highly hydrated dough can be challenging to prepare. If you struggle with shaping wet dough, only increase hydration until you can handle it.

Avoid Using Metal Bowls and Utensils

Sourdough making leads to acid production — acid and metal are not a good combination. The acid can corrode the metal (or poor-quality plastic), and the corroded material can seep into your bread.

Use high-quality plastic or wooden bowls for sourdough-making to avoid this potential health hazard. The same applies to utensils. Don't use anything made from steel, iron, or aluminum. Wood and silicone are fine but ensure the silicone is of good quality.

Adjust Oven Temperature for Higher Rise

As a first-time sourdough baker, you may prefer to err on the side of caution when setting your oven temperature and putting it on low. Most newbies do this because they're afraid to under-bake the bread from the inside or over-bake it from the outside.

Unfortunately, setting your oven temperature too low can prevent your dough from rising to its full height. Remember, during the first part of baking, your dough rises and expands as the bubbles quickly escape toward the surface. Higher temperatures allow it to rise more rapidly and evenly.

Pro Tip: Preheat your oven to the highest temperature setting and bake the bread for 20 minutes. This is enough for rising and crust formation. Then, turn the temperature down to cook the inner layers.

Stick with a Recipe

Mastering sourdough necessitates lots of patience and practice. Part of this is learning how to execute a recipe to perfection. You don't have to look for a new recipe merely because your bread didn't turn out as expected the first time.

Find a promising, recommended, proven recipe and stick with it until you can confidently make the perfect bread. Once you've mastered the recipe, you can look for new avenues for sourdough-based creations.

Besides, when you find a good way to make sourdough for the first time (one that works based on your needs and schedule), you should repeat your bake every time.

Sticking with the same recipe has another benefit: It helps you understand how sourdough behaves, which is crucial when learning the ins and outs of the process. Once you understand what your sourdough needs, you can alter the recipe, including using different flour, adding other ingredients, etc.

Chapter 6: Sourdough and Your Culinary Journey

You've come a long way on your culinary journey. You've learned what sourdough is, how to make and bake it, what bread you can make, and how to avoid common mistakes. It's time to take a step further and start another chapter in your budding sourdough journey. This chapter teaches you about incorporating sourdough into meals, making classic and unusual pairings, and showcasing your brand and bread-making skills in gatherings.

Incorporating Sourdough into Different Meals

Incorporating sourdough into meals can be an excellent first step when learning to use it in your cooking. Besides bread, you can use sourdough in your dishes in many ways. Here is how:

Pastas

Imagine having an easy meal of spaghetti Bolognese (or your favorite pasta dishes) — made better with sourdough pasta. You can have the sauce and the pasta prepared ahead of time on the weekends and have a homemade dish on busy weekdays. You can freeze the pasta if you make a large batch and thaw it when needed.

21. Even pasta can be made using sourdough. Source:
https://pixabay.com/photos/noodle-pasta-food-italian-1303003/

Another idea is spaghetti with meatballs made with sourdough. Instead of regular breadcrumbs, add crumbs made from your favorite sourdough loaf.

Like spaghetti, sourdough mac and cheese is another popular dish as it's equally easy to prepare. You can make this from scratch if you have a mature starter ready to be made into pasta dough. Pair the pasta with steamed veggies or fresh salad for more than a comfort meal or a quick meal for hungry children.

Soups

Soup on the side is not the only way to enjoy your sourdough bread. You can include sourdough dumplings in the soup. They can spruce up traditional soups, like vegetables or chicken, giving them a richer flavor that everyone will enjoy.

Savory Pies and Filled Rolls

Chicken pot pie is a wonderful comfort food, especially during colder nights. It can be prepared in advance, especially if you make it with sourdough. The dough's flavor and unique texture bring out the filling's complex aromas.

Pulled pork ciabatta rolls are ideal for a quick, easy meal. Again, you can make a large batch of sourdough rolls in advance and freeze them when you want to fill them with your favorite topping (pulled pork is only a suggestion).

Speaking of easy meals, tortillas are at the top of the list. When made from sourdough, you can fill them with anything and have a delicious meal ready in no time.

Casseroles and Fritters

A sourdough hash brown casserole is an excellent meal prep idea. As with all sourdough dishes (and those with potatoes), it's a fantastic side to a main dish.

Another meat-free combination idea is sourdough sweet potato and chickpea fritters. You can incorporate them into sourdough sandwiches, hamburger buns, or salads.

For dessert, you can try a sweet fritter, like a sourdough banana variant. Or a baked donut made from fluffy sourdough.

Burgers and Pizzas

It's not only the mature sourdough that makes delicious burger buns. Discards can be as useful and paired with almost any topping. If your discards are from a young starter, their sweeter taste complements stronger flavors like a cheese-meat combo. They'll go well with milder flavors like crispy chicken if they're from a more mature starter.

Do you want to step up your burger or sandwich-bread game? Bake cheese in your loaf. It will melt and add an irresistible taste to the dough.

Making sourdough pizza is a rewarding journey, even more so when the family joins in. If you have children, feel free to include them in the preparations. Let everyone choose their favorite toppings and see how these pair with sourdough. You only need a good sourdough pizza dough recipe, and once you learn how to make it, the sky's the limit for the topping combinations. Sweet, sour, pricey, savory, and cheesy are flavors you already have in your sourdough so it will bring them out from the toppings.

Pies and Cakes

If you enjoy ice cream and pie after dinner, you'll love it even more when the pie is made with a delicious sourdough crust. The latter is also excellent for quiche.

Or, if you prefer cakes, you can have a simple sourdough cake with tea after your meal. Fruit cakes are highly recommended as sourdough often pairs well with sweet and sour fruity flavors.

*22. Despite their unpopularity, sourdough pies are amazingly tasty.
Source: https://unsplash.com/photos/brown-pie-on-white-
ceramic-plate-2RXt6CQY_0c*

Roasts

What would be a roast dinner without gravy? Besides a sourdough loaf as a side, you can incorporate sourdough into your gravy. The secret is to use a small amount of the discards to thicken the sauce (instead of flour).

A suggestion for after the roast is sourdough popovers — they make scoping up the leftover gravy easy.

Breakfast

Discards are perfect for thickening pancake batter, whether for a breakfast of sourdough pancakes with syrup and fruit or a more elaborate dish like tempura chicken and veggies.

Sourdough cheese waffles will be a dream come true for waffle enthusiasts. Try sourdough zucchini muffins if you prefer muffins for breakfast or brunch.

Pairing Sourdough with Other Foods

The sky's the limit for pairing sourdough with other foods. If you don't know how to get started, below are a few suggestions:

Butters and Toasts

There is no denying that sourdough breads make perfect toast. However, why stop at plain toast when you can make French toast? You know what pairs well with sourdough French toast — fruit butter. Who knew combining eggs, bread, fruit, and dairy could make something so delicious?

Generally, sourdough bread goes well with fruit, especially if the dough is made a little less sour. Alternatively, you can layer your fruit on top of almond butter-covered bread.

Try a blackberry burrata toast for a unique taste. It's an unusual but more rewarding combination.

Try avocado toast if you prefer a savory combination. They are popular because they're easy, refreshing, and healthier with sourdough.

A more classic route is the breakfast or brunch evergreen eggs, mushrooms, cheese, and bread combo. Served warm, the melting cheesy topping will be the perfect pairing for traditional eggs served on bread.

Dips

While traditionally eaten with flatbread, hummus will be excellent with sourdough.

It's easy to make from scratch and perfectly complements the dough flavor.

Likewise, your sourdough creations will pair well with a classic Italian-style aromatic olive oil dip. The herbs in the oil will bring out the bread's nuanced aromas, while the oil enhances the crunchy-soft texture contrast.

Casseroles

Breakfast casserole with sourdough bread? Yes, it's the most customizable and delicious food you can begin your day with. Add whatever veggies, breakfast meats, and additional toppings you want for the perfect combination of flavors.

Did you know the classic, served with butter, fruits, etc., is only one of the many ways to eat French toast? For example, you can make it into a casserole and get a sweet treat like bread pudding. As a beginner whose loaves may not always turn out right, this is the perfect way to turn the tide and create something delicious.

Another tip for combining sourdough French toast is to make the ultimate comfort food — peanut butter and jelly French toast. It's hearty and is guaranteed to brighten your day.

Soups

You can't think about sourdough pairing without considering soups. For example, use your bread as a dip for carrot cauliflower soup for a yummy dose of vegetables and carb deliciousness.

You can make a spicy carrot and lentil soup for cold winter nights. Add a little vinegar to the soup for the perfect harmony with the sourdough bread. Alternatively, you can make caramelized onion soup (the more onion types you can add, the better), top it off with melted cheese, and par with crunchy sourdough bread.

Do you only have pantry staples available? No problem. With a hamburger soup paired with the perfect slice of sourdough bread, you can turn food as simple as beans, potatoes, tomatoes, and ground beef into a feast.

When in a hurry and tempted to open a can of chicken noodle soup, having a prepared pressure cooker homemade variant will save the day. It's healthier and pairs well with sourdough, which you can store for days.

Do you want to get someone to try asparagus (or try it yourself but aren't a fan)? Prepare a little sourdough bun as a side, and you might learn to love this soup. The same applies to cabbage, mushrooms, or vegetables you want to incorporate into your or your loved ones' diet. They will not say no to the sour bread, and once they try the bread dipped in the soups, they'll enjoy the flavors it brings out.

Spreads

Spreads made with tuna, chicken, or a cheesy veggie combination are a match made in heaven with sourdough bread's diverse flavor. A tuna spinach spread on crunchy sourdough can be the perfect combination, even for children (who may not be fans of leafy veggies).

Likewise, chimichurri chicken spreads add a new layer of flavor to the classic grilled cheese sourdough sandwich. Add bacon or turkey bacon, chutney, and pepper jack cheese for a more gourmet variation (because you can never have enough variants of grilled cheese).

A sweet smores spread will harmonize well with plain sourdough. Or, if you have more experience and want to experiment with your sweet daughter, try making chocolate chip cookie dough. You'll likely have all the ingredients during the colder months, so why not try making a new combination?

Salads

Salads are as classic to serve with sourdough bread as toast. Whether it's creamy tuna with croutons or a rotisserie chicken salad in a sandwich — a crossover between spreads and salads — pairing it with sourdough has plenty of benefits. It's easy and quick to make, light, and filling enough to entice you to make it again.

Meat Sauces

Why stop at meat spreads when you can make meat sauce? Warning: a creamy chipped beef sauce or a classic spaghetti sauce paired with sourdough bread can quickly become everyone's favorite.

Are you preparing for the holidays and want to incorporate sourdough recipes into time-honored dishes? Try making homemade sourdough stuffing. It's quick to make it on the same day, so you can focus on preparing other, more important aspects of the special days.

Showcasing Your Sourdough Skills at Gatherings

Once you learn to make delicious sourdough dishes for your enjoyment, you'll likely want to share them with others. Intertwining art and science, sourdough bread takes patience and practice to master. If you host gatherings for friends and family regularly, this will be the perfect time to highlight these skills and the show-stopping recipes you've added to your arsenal.

Another reason sourdough bread is a fantastic option for parties and similar functions is it stays fresh for much longer than industrial yeast-leavened bread. You can prepare the dishes ahead and serve them at your convenience.

Below are a few recommendations for showcasing your sourdough skills at gatherings:

Toasts

Garlic bread is an old-time party favorite, from brunches to evening receptions. The delicious creamy garlic spread pairs well with sourdough bread's tangy taste and will gain everyone's approval.

Do you know what else is likely to be approved at a party? Cheese. Adding a layer of melted cheese over buttered bread is one step over the classic garlic bread. Besides a standalone dish, it is a fantastic appetizer before a pasta dish at a family dinner.

You can't go wrong with the traditional flatbread. It's a tasty treat you can serve with many delectable toppings. Furthermore, it's super easy to prepare, so you don't have to spend hours in the kitchen before your gathering.

Another cheesy bread idea for gatherings is the pull-apart cheddar stuffed sourdough bread. The soft, gooey interior and the bread's crispy crunch exterior make it hard to resist pairing. Add some bacon and ranch for the perfect appetizer or brunch food.

While not technically a toast, bruschetta is also a flavorful appetizer. The sourdough bruschetta pairs well with sweet and savory foods like caramelized onions. Pile the soft and jammy onions on the crispy bread slices, and you'll have the perfect starter for a Mediterranean-themed party.

Crunchy Starters

Crostini makes delicious starters and they're quick to make. For example, a tomato and mozzarella crostini will instantly infuse your gathering with summer Italian vibes that are guaranteed to create a relaxing atmosphere. They are delightful, especially when made with toasted sourdough bread.

The soft, salty comfort food, pretzels, are especially great when soft on the inside and slightly crunchy on the outside. With a sourdough starter, this is how they'll be, and they are guaranteed to become a hit on game nights.

Make pretzel buns instead if you want to step it up a notch. You can use these for sliders and sandwiches, elevating the simple snack to a party appetizer level.

No matter how you use them, sourbread croutons are a great way to impress people during dinners and gatherings. Toasted golden brown, they taste much better than regular bread croutons, not to mention the store-bought, pre-made variety.

Do you have plenty of discards and are preparing a large party? Don't worry. You have the basis for the perfect party snack: pretzel bites. Be prepared to serve plenty of drinks, too, for all those thirsty people who can't resist the soft, salty treats.

Sandwiches

Open-faced sandwiches are another popular party food, and when made with sourdough bread, you can top them with almost everything. For example, you can pair them with eggs for a brunch or breakfast reception.

Mint-cucumber tomato sandwiches can be a great option if you're looking for a more refreshing sandwich. It is a level above the quintessential cucumber tea sandwich but doesn't require too much preparation time.

If you genuinely want to showcase how diverse sourdough can be, serving grilled cheese with ham and apple does the trick. It's sweet, savory, and tangy — and that's only the topping. Each note will find its pair among the sourdough flavors as it melts in your guests' mouths.

Dip Bowls

Are you tired of boring appetizer ideas and looking for something to spark conversation and your guests' appetites? Serve the appetizers in sourdough dip bowls. For a daytime event, serve a hammy, oniony, cheesy, creamy bowl in perfectly baked sourdough bread. Alternatively, you can make a creamy spinach dip. It will be a crowd-pleaser among vegetarians and vegans.

Prepare something that can be chilled and stored until serving for a nighttime gathering. A baked crab dip will harmonize perfectly with the complex flavors of the sourdough bread bowl you'll serve it in.

Sunday Brunch Casserole

Another idea for Sunday brunch is a casserole with everything you would use at a traditional Sunday breakfast — sausages, veggies, eggs, cheese, etc. It's hearty enough to serve several people, perfect for larger daytime gatherings.

Desserts and Other Sweet Sourdough Creations

Do you want to satisfy your guests' sweet tooth? Serve them a chocolate-filled sourdough brioche. It will be a hard-to-resist treat. It's crunchy on the outside and airy on the inside, and the chocolate melts in the mouth. What's not to love about it?

- Sourdough strawberry shortcake
- Sourdough thumbprint cookies
- Sugar cookie bars (or sugar cookies cut into specific shapes for themed events)
- Lemon poppy seed sourdough muffins
- Sourdough banana nut muffins

You can offer sourdough crepes, blueberry muffins, or sourdough oatmeal cookies for a healthier option for breakfast or brunch.

A sourdough cranberry bread is a twist on the classic banana bread and is perfect for keeping up the holiday spirit among your guests.

Sneak a little zucchini into your sweet sourdough bread recipe. It makes the dough tender and is a great way to get children to eat more veggies.

Chapter 7: Inspiring Stories and Testimonials

As tantalizing as the prospect of making your healthy bread is, the challenges of sourdough baking can be disheartening. Reading about other bakers' real-life experiences and success stories can inspire you to continue your journey without faltering.

Besides the stories from fellow sourdough enthusiasts, this chapter offers you advice for overcoming potential challenges and celebrating each successfully completed milestone as a tremendous victory.

Real-Life Experiences of Sourdough Enthusiasts

To some, bread baking is about returning to their roots and making food without unnecessary and often harmful ingredients.

Ana's Story

Growing up in the countryside, my love for homegrown and homemade food was inherently ingrained in my heart. However, after moving to a larger city, I was steering away from this way of life and relying on supermarkets for my food sources, including bread. One day, I read the ingredient list of the artificial bread I bought. I was quite surprised at how long it was.

Thinking back to my childhood, I remembered that, to make bread, you essentially needed flour and water. So, why would I eat all the other ingredients in the bread from the supermarket when it doesn't even taste as good as homemade bread? The answer was simple: I shouldn't. I stopped buying supermarket bread and started making simple, healthy bread.

Looking into what the healthiest bread option would be (and what does not require me to invest in fancy bread-making machines), I decided on sour bread. I knew one of my friends frequently made sourdough, so I reached out to her, asking her to teach me the basics. At the first session, I was in awe when we got to try to finish a loaf made by our hands, and it tasted far superior to industrially made bread.

I was aware of the challenges but realized I could do this at home. I asked my friend for a piece of her starter and embarked on my sourdough-making adventure.

It wasn't long before I became overwhelmed. It took time to figure out how to feed my starter, and the information about when and how to incorporate it into the recipes was confusing. Then, I made my starter from scratch, which only happened after several failed attempts. I was close to abandoning the project many times and questioned why I even dared to try it in the first place.

Fortunately, my friend and the helpful sourdough community I found online encouraged me to overcome those challenges. As I shared my passion and less-than-successful experiences, more and more people reached out to me with advice on improving.

One of the most useful pieces of advice I got is to write everything down. Documenting the steps I took with each sourdough-making process, I could go back and see where it went wrong or where I got it right. This helped me learn from my mistakes. Eventually, I learned not to kill my starter right after making it (yes, I struggled even with that in the beginning), feeding my starter became easier, and those lumpy, flat loaves became quite decent-looking.

I'm still learning as I understand that making sourdough bread at home takes lots of patience and practice. Still, I can now revel in the amazing feeling of making my own bread and sharing the sourdough goodness with my family and friends.

Dylan's Story

Others find the process interesting but seemingly too complicated — until they try it and fall in love with it.

I've always been fascinated with bread-making, but it was so elusive that it took me a long time to make my own bread. My family had plenty of great cooks and bakers, but I never mastered their recipes.

When I first researched how to make sourdough bread, I was confused. It seemed to require few ingredients, but the timeline was very long, and the steps, such as feeding, proofing, shaping, etc., were not something I thought I would be comfortable doing.

Ultimately, I chose to take on this challenge and start the project because I had time. I figured that time was the only thing I had to lose. If it didn't work out, I would know that breadmaking is not one of my strong suits. For a while, I felt this was what I was proving to myself precisely, except I wasn't. I was proving to myself that I could do it.

I became passionate about the process, which fueled my need to learn new techniques. My first loaves were not great, but they became better. The taste was not too bad, but I could get the texture right. Yet, I was doing it — I was baking, and I continued to bake. Then, I made my first "perfect" loaf of sourdough bread (to me, it was perfect, which is what counts).

While I was skeptical about how successful the continuation of my journey would be, I had confidence that I could be triumphant — and I was. After a hauntingly slow start, the process becomes easier. Maintaining my commitment (and a sense of humor) helped a lot because there were plenty of times when things didn't go as planned. When this happened, I pivoted and turned to another avenue. For example, when the bread I made didn't quite have the intended texture, I looked up another recipe and found a way to use the bread as best as possible.

I learned that sourdough-making can be flexible. At first, I was worried about how I would manage the feeding and bread-making steps. However, the more I baked, the more I understood how to adapt everything to fit my schedule. Initially, your starter may require daily attention, but you learn to maintain a healthy starter without checking on it several times a day once you get the hang of it.

I love that I can adapt sourdough to my schedule and my recipes. The dough doesn't always have to taste sour, so you have leeway – also, the complex flavor or the naturally leavened bread pairs well with many foods. Then, there are the discards that don't even require proofing, so I can use them to whip up a starter-based meal in no time.

Zoe's Story

Some people are attracted to the meditative appeal of bread-making.

When I first encountered the bread-making trend on social media, I hadn't thought of making my own bread. I admired those who took the time and energy to create their (often intricately scored) homemade loaves. However, I felt this was too much hassle.

What ultimately changed my mind was the rising food prices. I had to fork over more and more money if I wanted to eat healthier bread. So, one day, I thought, "What if I invested my time into bread-making instead of my money into bread-buying?" Instead of spending my free time scrolling through social media, I read up and experimented with making sourdough starters.

Surprisingly, the slow, methodical process of measuring ingredients, nurturing my starter, and preparing it for baking wasn't as daunting as I initially thought. It helped that I took a professional baker's advice and began my journey with a ready-made dehydrated starter.

I went from reviving this ready-made dehydrated starter to baking several loaves of sourdough bread in a month. During this time, plenty of flour and sweat was spilled, not to mention more than half of the loaves were not picture-worthy. I added these to my never-ending supply of discards and used them for meals I never thought of incorporating sourdough into.

I noticed how much I enjoyed learning new techniques and recipes and how much calmer it made me feel. If you disregard the math part, everything else flows naturally. You feed the starter, make the dough, leave it to rise, and bake. There is a lot of repetition, which I find soothing — it's like a unique meditation. Except here, I get to create something healthy and delicious.

Making sourdough makes me let go of control, which feels like heaven. Dealing with unpredictable factors is humbling. It taught me that everything isn't about perfection and productivity. Yes, making my bread makes me feel productive. However, I feel this way because I know I'm doing something I enjoy.

Overcoming Challenges and Celebrating Successes

The many challenges you'll encounter on your sourdough-making journey can make you feel you'll never become successful in this art. Yet, between those challenges, you'll also have many victories worth celebrating, no matter how small they might be.

So, the first loaf you baked didn't turn out quite right. To get there, you had to nurture your starter carefully, which you've accomplished. You can tick off these from your learning list and focus on understanding what went wrong with the rest of the process. You can always give it another go. Persistence is key.

Remember, you're embarking on a long process of creating something natural to make sourdough. You won't have the aid of industrial ingredients to make everything come out perfect. Conversely, the process is more rewarding. You're learning to manipulate a natural and wide process, which is a victory.

Once you make your first starter from scratch, remember you made this wonder from only two ingredients: water and flour. You achieved these two components to start a myriad of chemical processes and reactions, resulting in an active starter. Isn't that great?

Every time you make bread successfully, make it a goal to get the next one to be as good (not failing the same recipe will be a small victory). Then, once your bread from the same recipe is always on par with the last one, you can make it a challenge to create something better by slightly altering the recipe. You can try new recipes once you've achieved this. However, as beginners, it's always a good idea to stick with one recipe and persevere until you master it.

If you aren't used to waiting for your culinary projects to ripen, exercising patience while your dough becomes ready will be another triumph. Many beginners make the mistake of using a starter before it's ready. If you do, you won't repeat the same error next time. Likewise, you learn that if the dough doesn't spring back after proofing, it's not ready to bake. Otherwise, you'll end up with a dense loaf. Getting through each milestone requires patience and willingness to learn what went wrong. Once you do, they'll be worth celebrating.

How can you celebrate these successes? Sharing them with friends and family would be one option. While waiting for your first successful dough to get ready, why not make something out of the discards? You'll have plenty of these and should learn how to use them effectively. There are plenty of recipes for discards, and incorporating sourdough into your meals is quite easy.

Do you know someone on a similar culinary journey or who is already baking sourdough regularly? If so, share your discards with them. Ask them what they think of your sourdough's flavor and texture. Getting positive feedback can be incredibly encouraging and will give you something to look forward to when your dough becomes bake-ready.

Whether it's a new recipe or an old one you want to improve or alter, getting simple steps right can feel victorious. You'll deal with arbitrary conditions like humidity, temperature, microbial diversity, etc. These affect how your sourdough turns out. Even if you use the same filtered water at just the right temperature and the same carefully sifted flour, your bread may still turn out slightly different.

When changing ratios, you're adding another variable. The result will be far more different than you thought, which is normal and part of the learning journey.

Perhaps surprisingly, one of the hardest steps to master is kneading. Sourdough is incredibly resistant, so you can't overcome it. The challenge is not to leave it under-kneaded. Fortunately, there are several techniques to use. For example, you can alternate between classical kneading and turning and folding. Once the 10-15 minutes of kneading becomes automatic (along with the fermentation period between the repeated kneading sessions and the proofing afterward) and you have a springy and bubbly dough, it's time for another victory dance.

Proofing might not be a challenge, but it is a nuisance. You've gone through days of starter feeding and hours of kneading and shaping, and now you must wait several more hours before your dough is ready to bake. One way to overcome this challenge is to time the beginning of the proofing for early evening. Start at room temperature, then finish it in the fridge overnight. By morning, you'll have a ready-to-go dough — just in time for breakfast or brunch delicacies.

Once you take your freshly baked sourdough bread out of the oven and slice it into a masterpiece with the perfect crunchy texture, you'll realize all the hard work was worth it. The satisfaction you get from creating something so special is unparalleled.

Whether your passion for baking is newfound or you haven't tried making sourdough before, you'll find the journey as exhilarating as it is surprising. Some of these surprises may be negative and frustrating. You may even find an aspect you thought was easy or challenging. However, you'll keep pursuing your goal of creating the perfect loaf with will and determination.

Over time, you'll intuitively understand your starter's finicky temperament. Your skill set will grow, and so will your patience. You'll rise victorious in battles against dense texture and conquer quests for the ultimate crumb perfection.

There will be despair among these trumps, but none should indicate the end of your journey. They are merely bumps in the road toward growing as a sourdough baking artist.

Each failure teaches you a valuable lesson. Sometimes, it will be up to you to discover what lesson you are meant to learn despite all the available resources. Remember, sourdough making is a mixture of art and science. Science will give you the ingredients for the results, and art gives you the tools to interpret them.

Not all results have to be flawless; understanding this is part of overcoming your baking challenges. Your bread doesn't have to look aesthetically pleasing to taste good. Achieving the latter without the former is a victory in a major battle. You've created something healthy and better tasting than the blend of industrially made products. Isn't that worth celebrating?

Hidden within each success is the potential to create something even better. Be determined to unlock it, and you'll be rewarded with a purpose, satisfaction, and improved well-being.

To those embarking on this eventful journey, don't be discouraged by your failures. Instead, celebrate the little victories, even if your victory is figuring out what went wrong. It gives you the power to do better next time, so it's an enormous step toward mastery.

The perfect sourdough bread may seem unattainable for a while, but you'll get closer with each attempt. Remain determined and nurture your passion as you nurture your starter. Ultimately, your efforts will yield a victorious bread that will make you and everyone you share it with proud.

Conclusion

You have reached the end of your baking experience with *"Sourdough Starter for Beginners."* You should feel more equipped and ready to start your sourdough adventure. This book has given you the best knowledge, expertise, recipes, confidence, and inspiration to become the best sourdough baking genius. You have learned a lot. Here are the takeaways from the book:

You learned about sourdough's great history and science and took your time to understand fermentation fully. You learned how to create a live culture to leaven your bread instead of commercial yeast. This gives sourdough bread its unique flavor and texture and many great nutritional benefits.

You explored the essential ingredients and tools necessary to make your sourdough bread. This book discussed the importance of high-quality, unbleached flour, flour types, and suitable water. You learned how a healthy starter becomes the core of your sourdough recipes.

The book explored how to properly care for your sourdough and maintain it by feeding and discarding it. You learned about feeding schedules, what makes a healthy starter, and keeping a stable environment for your starter to stay healthy and alive. In the following chapters, you learned the basic sourdough bread recipe that prepared you for the more expert-level recipes.

Then, you mastered more complex recipes, such as making pizzas, flatbreads, and sweet treats. These recipes come with healthy tips to support your baking adventure. This guide contains troubleshooting advice to help you manage the stresses and challenges you may face in your sourdough baking journey. Practical solutions were provided for your benefit.

Sourdough baking is a one-of-a-kind experience from which you will learn something new every time. Bakers have practiced this art for centuries, and it holds deep value in every baker's heart. It is okay to make mistakes. Keep yourself open to the possibility of learning from every step or misstep.

The aim was to make this beginner-friendly so that all readers can grasp sourdough baking skills without complications. Please don't forget to leave an excellent review for this guide if you found this book helpful in your journey as a sourdough baker. Your feedback will help improve this book for future readers.

May your journey be full of exciting recipes and beautiful moments, sharing them with your loved ones. Happy baking!

References

admin. (2024, April 11). 20+ Sourdough Bread Appetizers. Starters and Treats. https://startersandtreats.com/20-sourdough-bread-appetizers/

Adney, I. (n.d.). How this baker went from sourdough enthusiast to a six-figure, New York Times bestselling author. ConvertKit. https://convertkit.com/resources/creator-stories/maurizio-leo

Anja. (2019, January 24). How to Make Sourdough Starter From Scratch. Our Gabled Home. https://ourgabledhome.com/how-to-make-your-own-sourdough-starter-from-scratch/

Anja. (2023, October 30). How To Know When Your Sourdough Starter Is Ready. Our Gabled Home. https://ourgabledhome.com/how-to-know-when-your-sourdough-starter-is-ready/

Avery, M. (2023). Sourdough home. Sourdough Home. https://www.sourdoughhome.com/water/

Ballis, S. (2022, April 1). The 13 Most Common Sourdough Bread Mistakes. Allrecipes. https://www.allrecipes.com/article/sourdough-mistakes/

Bandurski, K. (2024, May 5). 36 Recipes That Start With Sourdough Bread. Taste of Home. https://www.tasteofhome.com/collection/recipes-with-sourdough-bread/

Bass, L. (2021, December 31). Maintaining and Feeding A Sourdough Starter. Farmhouse on Boone. https://www.farmhouseonboone.com/how-to-care-for-sourdough-starter/

Bass, L. (2022, January 28). Sourdough Scoring - How To Make Beautiful Sourdough Bread. Farmhouse on Boone. https://www.farmhouseonboone.com/sourdough-scoring-how-to-make-beautiful-sourdough-bread/

Bass, L. (2024, March 6). Beginner's sourdough bread recipe. Farmhouse on Boone. https://www.farmhouseonboone.com/beginners-sourdough-bread-recipe/

Bespoke Bread. (2023, March 1). What is Sourdough—Why Do People Love It? Bespoke Bread. https://bespokebread.sg/blogs/news/what-is-sourdough-why-do-people-love-it

Chef Roberto. (2023, September 29). Sourdough Timeline: Understanding the Fermentation Process - The Sourdough Science Academy. Thesourdoughscience.com. https://thesourdoughscience.com/sourdough-timeline-understanding-the-fermentation-process/

Chin, T. (2023, June 2). How to knead, fold, and shape sourdough bread. Serious Eats. https://www.seriouseats.com/sourdough-how-to

Chin, T. (2024, June 22). The Science of Sourdough Starters. Serious Eats. https://www.seriouseats.com/sourdough-starter-science

Clark, M. (2023, October 6). Why Sourdough Over Other Breads? Living Well; Living Well. https://www.livingwellwithmandy.com/post/why-sourdough-over-other-breads

Duska, A. (2023a, January 18). Essential tools for sourdough bread baking. Little Spoon Farm. https://littlespoonfarm.com/essential-tools-equipment-for-sourdough-bread-baking/

Duska, A. (2023b, October 3). How to make sourdough starter. Little Spoon Farm. https://littlespoonfarm.com/sourdough-starter-recipe/

Duska, A. (2024, June 27). sourdough chocolate chip cookies. Little Spoon Farm. https://littlespoonfarm.com/sourdough-chocolate-chip-cookies-recipe/#recipe

Editor. (2023, November 9). Interview With @SourdoughBrandon From Massachusetts, United States. The Sourdough People. https://sourdoughbread.ca/sourdoughbrandon

Hamel, P. (2015, October 29). Adding sourdough to a recipe | King Arthur Baking. Www.kingarthurbaking.com. https://www.kingarthurbaking.com/blog/2015/10/29/adding-sourdough-recipe

Hamel, P. (2021, October 25). Here's how I streamline my sourdough baking | King Arthur Baking. Www.kingarthurbaking.com. https://www.kingarthurbaking.com/blog/2021/10/15/how-to-streamline-your-sourdough-bread-baking

Jennibee. (2023, November 6). Sourdough discard pancake muffins. Jennibeemine. https://jennibeemine.com/sourdough-discard-pancake-muffin-bites/

Kimbell, V. (2023, October 4). Fermentation explained. The Sourdough Club. https://thesourdoughclub.com/fermentation-explained/

Leo, M. (2015, November 27). Sourdough Starter Maintenance Routine | The Perfect Loaf. Www.theperfectloaf.com. https://www.theperfectloaf.com/sourdough-starter-maintenance-routine/

Leo, M. (2021, May 27). How do I feed my sourdough starter? | The Perfect Loaf. Www.theperfectloaf.com. https://www.theperfectloaf.com/how-do-i-feed-my-sourdough-starter/

Leo, M. (2024, July 2). Beginner's sourdough bread. The Perfect Loaf. https://www.theperfectloaf.com/beginners-sourdough-bread/

Leo, M. (2024a, April 9). 21 common sourdough starter problems with solutions. The Perfect Loaf. https://www.theperfectloaf.com/21-common-sourdough-starter-problems-with-solutions/

Leo, M. (2024b, May 2). Making an incredible sourdough starter from scratch in 7 easy steps. The Perfect Loaf. https://www.theperfectloaf.com/7-easy-steps-making-incredible-sourdough-starter-scratch/

Mama, T. P. (2023, January 3). How To Keep Sourdough Starter Warm. The Pantry Mama. https://www.pantrymama.com/how-to-keep-sourdough-starter-warm/

Mama, T. P. (2023, November 22). A Week of Dinner Ideas Using Sourdough Starter. The Pantry Mama. https://www.pantrymama.com/sourdough-dinner-ideas/

McCarthy, A. (2024, March 12). Sourdough Is Having a Moment… Again. Eater. https://www.eater.com/24094642/sourdough-bread-trending-again

Mel. (2024, March 28). Easy sourdough flatbread. Mel's Kitchen Cafe. https://www.melskitchencafe.com/easy-sourdough-flatbread/

Raffa, E. (2023, November 25). Artisan sourdough bread with all-purpose flour {soft, crisp & chewy!}. The Clever Carrot. https://www.theclevercarrot.com/2020/04/artisan-sourdough-with-all-purpose-flour/

Raffa, E. (2023, October 2). Crispy sourdough pizza crust (no steel or stone!). The Clever Carrot. https://www.theclevercarrot.com/2022/11/best-sourdough-pizza-crust-no-baking-steel-or-stone/

Raffa, E. (2024a, January 13). Best sourdough pancakes. The Clever Carrot. https://www.theclevercarrot.com/2020/05/homemade-fluffy-sourdough-pancakes/

Raffa, E. (2024a, January 13). Troubleshooting your sourdough starter. The Clever Carrot. https://www.theclevercarrot.com/2018/03/troubleshooting-your-sourdough-starter/

Raffa, E. (2024b, July 1). Beginner Sourdough starter recipe. The Clever Carrot. https://www.theclevercarrot.com/2019/03/beginner-sourdough-starter-recipe/

Raffa, E. (2024b, July 6). Sourdough bread: A beginner's guide. The Clever Carrot. https://www.theclevercarrot.com/2014/01/sourdough-bread-a-beginners-guide/

Real Bread Campaign. (2023, September 6). Real Bread in a virtual world: How Andra Stefanescu's online sourdough teaching business began and continues to develop. | Real Bread Campaign. Www.sustainweb.org. https://www.sustainweb.org/realbread/articles/sep23-real-bread-in-a-virtual-world-sourdough-explained/

Real Country 101.3. (n.d.). The Journey to the Perfect Sourdough: Embracing Frustration and the Art of Persistence | 101.3 Real Country. Https://1013realcountry.com/. https://1013realcountry.com/the-journey-to-the-perfect-sourdough-embracing-frustration-and-the-art-of-persistence/

Sage, K. (2021, August 13). Which type of flour to use for sourdough bread. Barley & Sage. https://www.barleyandsage.com/which-type-of-flour-to-use-for-sourdough-bread/#types-of-flour

Stafford, A. (2023, February 18). Essential tools and equipment for sourdough baking. Alexandra's Kitchen. https://alexandracooks.com/2019/11/05/essential-equipment-for-sourdough-bread-baking/

Stafford, A. (2024, June 26). Simple sourdough pizza crust: Step-by-step guide. Alexandra's Kitchen. https://alexandracooks.com/2020/05/01/simple-sourdough-pizza-a-step-by-step-guide/

Stephanie. (2019, March 28). sourdough baking tips and resources. Girl versus Dough. https://www.girlversusdough.com/sourdough-baking-tips/

Sullivan, K. (2020, May 15). The Challenge That Is Sourdough. Kingsley Sullivan. https://www.kingsleysullivan.com/post/the-challenge-that-is-sourdough

Tiffany. (2022, September 26). 40 Ways To Serve and Eat Sourdough Bread. Growing Dawn. https://growingdawn.com/40-ways-to-serve-and-eat-sourdough-bread/

Unveiling the Science Behind Sourdough Magic. (2023, December 14). Harvest Baking. https://harvestbaking.co/blogs/news/unveiling-the-science-behind-sourdough-magic

Vermontfoodlibrarian. (2024, April 14). Sourdough pancakes, muffins, and sweet breads. Vermont Food Librarian. https://vtfoodlib.com/category/sourdough-pancakes-muffins-and-sweet-breads/

Why Sourdough Bread is Valuable – Cotati Food Service. (2024). Cotatifoodservice.com. https://cotatifoodservice.com/why-sourdough-bread-is-valuable/

You Knead Sourdough. (n.d.). Top 10 Tips & Tricks for Making Sourdough. You Knead Sourdough. https://www.youkneadsourdough.com.au/blogs/sourdough-stories/top-10-tips-tricks-for-making-sourdough

Made in the USA
Las Vegas, NV
03 January 2025

15779083R00066